COVENTRY'S
BLITZ

COVENTRY'S
BLITZ

DAVID MCGRORY

AMBERLEY

To those who gave their testimonies and those that lived and died in Coventry in those dangerous days.

Frontispiece: Normal life continues. A view looking across the devastation from Jordan Well to St Michael and Holy Trinity church taken on 14 April 1941.

First published 2015

Amberley Publishing
The Hill, Stroud
Gloucestershire, GL5 4EP

www.amberley-books.com

British Library Cataloguing in Publication Data.
A catalogue record for this book is available from the British Library.

ISBN 978 1 4456 4999 3 (print)
ISBN 978 1 4456 5000 5 (ebook)

Typesetting and Origination by Amberley Publishing.
Printed in Great Britain.

Contents

Acknowledgements

I would like to thank all those who contributed to this work (their names appear in the text). The information was gathered over many years, so some are no longer with us, but their memories live on. Also I would like to thank Rob Orland (see Historic Coventry website), John Ashby, David Larkin, Maurice Rattigan, Tony Rose and West Midlands Police, Fred Jennings, Coventry Local Studies Centre, *Coventry Evening Telegraph*, British Library.

Many thanks to the following for photographs: Roger Bailey, Fred Jennings, Maurice Burnell, Olive Eades, James Armer, Bill Tisdale, Les Fannon, Midland Air Museum, *Coventry Evening Telegraph* and the David McGrory Collection.

Abbreviations

ARP   Air Raid Precautions
DA   Delayed Action (bomb)
HE   High Explosive
MDT *Midland Daily Telegraph*
UXB Unexploded Bomb
AFS   Auxillary Fire Service
FAP   First Aid Post

Foreword

For many, the blitz in Coventry is thought of as being the night of 14/15 November 1940. Although this was Coventry's worst night of bombing, it was, however, not the only night the city received attention from German bombers. Although no other raids matched this for ferocity, there were in total forty-one actual raids on Coventry and 371 siren alerts. These constant alerts led to many leaving the city on a nightly basis, heading into the nearby countryside, seeking shelter in farms, barns and even pigsties! Some bought tickets on coaches which took them out of the city, and parked up in a field for the night. The dark isolation of the countryside offered the safety that built-up target Coventry couldn't!

The Second World War in Coventry was an exceptionally busy period, as in the Second World War the city was a centre of war production with Whitleys, Wellingtons and Lancasters being made by Armstrong Whitworth in Baginton. Other firms, like Standard, more used to making cars, built 1,066 classic Mosquito fighter bombers. Being a centre of war production, in the early days of the war shadow factories were built on the outskirts of the city. These appear to have managed to get through this difficult period, but not without the aid of a little camouflage. Although Coventry made a lot more than planes, this was the excuse Goering gave for targeting the heart of the city on 14 November.

That raid on 14 November 1940 would change the city forever; few streets within the modern ring-road bear much resemblance to pre-1940 Coventry. But it wasn't all down to Hitler; much of the city was destroyed by planners. Donald Gibson was made city architect in 1938, and two weeks after the November raid said, 'The bombing of Coventry has given us a chance to rebuild a dignified and fitting city centre. Many citizens,' he told the Royal Society of Arts in London, 'had despaired of this possibility. High land values, the delays involved by town planning legislation, together with a lack of a plan for the central area, made it seem impossible. Now in a night, this is all changed; instead of a tightly-packed mass of buildings of every description, there are many burnt-out ruins and much desolation, debris and ashes, but like a forest fire the present evil may bring forth greater riches and beauty.' That tightly packed mass of buildings dating back centuries was much loved by Coventrians! But, less than two years earlier, Gibson had already begun designing a new city centre, which would destroy many old buildings, the process had already started! His comment of 1941 to the Architectural Association in London said it all. 'Post-war buildings,' he said, 'should be built to last no more than thirty years.'

Coventry is odd in the fact that much is modern but still in our daily lives we live with its past. The days that are covered in this book shaped the Coventry we live in today; we live with the results and consequences of those days, when the city was pummelled by bombs and was shaped, and still is shaped, by councils and various architects who add their little bit to that tightly packed mass of modern buildings.

Shelter

Many assume that when the glass was removed from Coventry Cathedral and St Mary's Hall in January 1940 it showed people were thinking ahead. Not the case, for few actually realise that we were preparing for war in Coventry as early as 6 August 1938. Over a year before the war officially started for us, Coventry housed one of the largest stores in the country of gas masks. From these stores Coventry had 220,000 masks issued by the ARP service, readying the city for gas attack. It was said at the time, 'Every person in the city within a period of twelve hours will receive a mask.' The following month every household in the city received a visit from the ARP to check if everyone had a mask. This was followed on 30 September throughout the city by a test black-out. Air raid wardens numbering 1,400 toured their patches to see the black-out was effectively adhered to.

In September 1938 between five and six hundred men began work digging air raid trenches in Spencer Park, Memorial Park, Stivichall Common, Primrose Hill Park, Radford Recreation Ground, Moseley Avenue, Naul's Mill Park, Radford Common, Edgewick Recreation Ground, Hearsall Common, Whitley Common, Binley Road, Barras Heath, Longford Recreation Ground, Gosford Green, Livingstone Road, Cheylesmore Estate (above Quinton Pool), Bird Street, Holbrook Lane, Foleshill Park, Holbrook Lane, Greyfriar's Green and Corporation Street. The first to be completed was a 600 capacity shelter on Greyfriar's Green. These first trenches were built to protect against gas and bullets – basically deep trenches with plank roofs covered in soil. These were quickly found to be inadequate and were soon concrete lined and covered, making them into the shelters better known today.

By 14 November 1940 the National Emergency Committee had created enough trench, basement and surface shelters in Coventry to accommodate 170,344 citizens. Also, in the beginning of September 1939, it is reported that, 'sandbagging continues apace' and that Anderson Shelters were being delivered to all areas by the truck load.

Available air raid shelter spaces by 13 September 1939 numbered in the low thousands, examples being a 200 capacity shelter under Radford Common, a 612 capacity shelter on Stivichall Common, a 550 capacity shelter under Edgewick Recreation Ground and a 400 capacity basement shelter under the Corporation's Leicester Row Depot.

War was declared on 3 September 1939, and fifteen-year-old Brenda Mendenhall, then of Sherlock Street, was home alone; she left school at fourteen to look after the family home. On the day war was declared, her father was away; he had taken her siblings down to her grandparents in Surrey. Brenda recalled, 'So I was alone, I looked up the garden, expecting any minute that the Germans would come walking down the path, then common sense prevailed.'

During the so called 'Phoney War', when little happened, children began to be evacuated to nearby towns such as Kenilworth and Leamington and further afield. Harry James recalls,

I was six years old and taken in by a farming family called Liggins at Long Marston. I recall being unable to sleep or eat for a few days but the lady must have realised and made an effort to comfort me. Soon I began to enjoy seeing cows, pigs, sheep and riding on the farmer's cart into nearby Broadway. One night I was woken up by loud bangs in the sky and what I now know was Coventry and Birmingham were being bombed. Then one day my Dad rode all the way from Coventry on his bike to fetch me home! I had my gas mask, ration book, identity card and I remember the lady wiping her eyes and waving goodbye!

Mrs Wellman of Wyken recalled,

I remember father fitting shutters in our house to stop any light showing, I was nineteen when war started. We were issued with ration books, identity cards and gas masks. We had no sweets, about 1/10*d* of meat each, two grams of butter, tea and sugar a week. If we went out for tea anywhere we had to take some of our food with us. We didn't see a banana for years. Very often we would have to queue for bread.

Of these early days Martin Hammond recalled,

At the outbreak of war I was ten years old and lived at No. 239 St George's Road. My first recollections were of the issuing of gas masks and the arrival of Anderson air raid shelters. We all had to carry our masks wherever we went in little brown cardboard boxes strung around our necks. Every now and again these had to be tested for faults by a piece of cardboard being put over the air intake, while we breathed in. The Anderson shelter had to be dug into the back garden and this was a job our father did and we kids held the parts in place while he bolted them together. Next he had to scrounge old wooden boxes from the local grocers,

Sometimes Andersons worked, sometimes they didn't; this one in Somerset Road, Radford, taken in 1941 obviously did!

which were filled with earth and built around the entrance as protection against bomb blast. It was all a waste of time as it was always flooded from a railway embankment, which was behind our garden, so we never used it.

Andersons were either cherished by families or hated; many were utilised after the war as garden sheds and some survive today ... they saved many lives. Doreen Earl remembered such an event:

We were in the Anderson shelter at the bottom of the garden one night during a raid and the house got a direct hit. If we had been inside we would all have been killed. My dad was really upset because he had left his false teeth upstairs in the house when we went to the shelter!

Some Andersons were never used, as a common problem was that they became permanently flooded with water. Many were just damp, as Doreen recalls:

It was very confined and damp. You had to keep your back straight and sit up because you couldn't lean on the damp walls, so it gave you backache after a while. There was almost no light, perhaps a couple of candles and no heating, so you got very cold sitting in the winter.

There were other alternatives such as the Morrison Shelter, which consisted of a steel cage placed under a heavy table. Pat Pittaway remembers them well for another reason:

> Some people had a shelter inside the house which was just an iron table, which you got underneath. I knew a family in Edgewick Road who had one. When I was a little girl I used to do tap dancing and would dance on top of this iron table in my tap shoes to entertain everyone, because it made a loud noise.

Then of course there was the old standby, the 'bogey hole', the cupboard under the stairs. As this was at the centre of the house it quite often survived; many elderly people preferred the bogey hole!

Back in the street, Martin Hammond recalls their shelter:

> Thankfully they built brick shelters in the street. It was early in the war that our father, who was on the reserve, was called up, even though he had done four years in the First World War. These brick shelters in the street gave us children another place to play and us boys used to dare others to jump from one shelter to the next, which were about six feet apart and seven or eight feet high. The re-enforced concrete slab on the top was thought to be dangerous if the single brick walls caved in, as it did in the next street and killed a boy. Every now and again the Home Guard appeared in the street and district doing training against the regular army. At one time I remember it was the Canadians in opposition. Tutton's Garage on the Humber Road was turned into a fire station. This was opposite our school, Folly Lane, and after lessons we used to go over and fill sand bags to protect the place from bomb blast. At the same time the council were digging up the playing fields on Humber Road to make deep shelters for the public. I think we went down these a few times during school air raid practice, but later on they became flooded and unusable. To make life a bit more comfortable during the many nights in the brick street shelter we put a carpet on the bare road below and had a couple of chairs and a table. There was a 2-foot by 2-foot hole connecting two halves of the shelter, the other half used by neighbours. We put a blanket across this for privacy, also a blanket across the front opening, for the blackout. At this time the nights were very dark because of the blackout and we all used to carry hand torches. They came in handy when delivering papers and to see other people in the street.

Public Shelters were not always good, for it was reported in August 1940 that:

> Stories of rowdyism and drunkenness in public air raid shelters in Coventry are causing concern to the police and ARP officials. According to some people, women and children in the shelters had been terrorised by drunken brawls and fights, even

Surface shelters survived in this Coventry Street, notice the blast has gone to the right, the buildings on the left, including the windows, are amazingly untouched.

during actual air raids ... Only threats of personal violence or forcible ejection from the shelters restore peace, and then only until the police officers have left ... then trouble quickly breaks out again.

Thankfully, over time, these problems died out as local men held the peace.

By 6 August 1938 the city had been divided into six ARP zones, the whole of the city had been mapped in detail and the six zones subdivided into twelve to twenty sectors depending on size. Coventry newspapers reported on 20 May 1939 that sixty-six Air Raid Precaution posts had been established and it was anticipated that 195 posts would be the final total. Posts were spread all over the city: in Radford School; Hare & Hounds Hotel, Keresley; the Brookville Theatre, Holbrook Lane; Wyken Pippin, Ansty Road; Burnt Post Hotel; and Westwood Heath School to name but a few. One month before this appeared, the *Alfred Herbert News* reported:

A successful excavation exercise was carried out on the 22 March. The whole of the office staff, pattern shop and various foundries, a total of 1,260 people,

ARP men from Holbrooks, Radford and Keresley pose in 1940; my own granddad is at the rear on the right.

were evacuated to the trenches at the back of the offices. The time taken from the sounding of the air raid alarm signal to the last person safely in the trench was under five minutes...

Herbert's led the city and many other factories quickly followed their lead.

Around this time other services were set up: First Aid Posts, First Aid Parties, ambulance service and casualty clearing stations at the Coventry and Warwickshire Hospital and Gulson Road Hospital. By August, 410 men and 1,200 women had been recruited. Also, women were being asked to train as auxiliary nurses. At this time a number of first aid posts had been established in the city at Gulson Rd Clinic, Old School Clinic, King St, Foleshill Baths, Barker Butts School, Allesley School, Centaur Road School, Whoberley School, Green Lane School, Wyken School, and the Out Patients Dept of the Coventry and Warwickshire Hospital.

In late February 1939 a recruiting office for No. 917 Barrage Balloon Squadron, which would cover Coventry, opened at 23 Hertford Street. The headquarters would later move to Cow Lane. The idea of the barrage was to try to force enemy planes to fly high above their intended targets to essentially make them less effective, especially in the case of precision bombing. The barrage would essentially make a difference and many could be seen around the city, some encircling industrial sites. The

An FAP (First Aid Post) with their ambulances, somewhere in Holbrooks in 1941.

hydrogen filled balloons were fixed to winches by steel cables, some permanently fixed, others mobile. They were served originally by teams of ten men, but later also teams of young women. The first barrage balloon was demonstrated by a London squadron in the War Memorial Park in March 1939. These great silver 'jumbos', as they were often called, surrounded the city and caused much consternation when they broken their moorings, dragging steel cables across rooftops before finally coming to rest in a side street or even on one occasion in Broadgate!

Olive Eades recalled to me in recent years that,

I joined the Women's Auxiliary Air Force on 23 December 1941, twelve days before my eighteenth birthday... We came to Coventry in April 1942 and were taken to Site 19, which was located on the common ground triangle at the junction of Tamworth and Keresley Green roads. There was a sixteen member crew plus a sergeant and a corporal. We were completely self-contained, rations were sent from Flight Headquarters daily and cooking was done on a rota basis. We did two hours guard duty, day and night, besides maintaining and operating the balloon, renewing and repairing equipment, making grommets, rope and wire splicing. The winch was a converted RAF lorry, operated by a crew member, which powered the cable reel to control the balloon's altitude. Everyone had their particular station which differed from time to time.

Olive Eades and the ladies of Site 19 taken in 1943.

A rare, but blurry, photograph of the first barrage balloon in the city being demonstrated in the War Memorial Park.

Of the balloon itself, she continued:

> A balloon was 62 feet long and over 25 feet in diameter. The top half was inflated
> with hydrogen which we kept topped up from gas bottles on the site. The bottom
> half, fins and rudder were filled with air. From the top down one side there was an
> aperture panel which was fixed by ripcord to a unit containing a cartridge. If the
> balloon broke away, the ripcord would pull the safety panel off to release the gas.
> When the balloon was not flying it was moored and had to be positioned 'nose
> into the wind' all the time. When the wind changed, we had to move the balloon,
> which was no joke when a gale was blowing!

Of their quarters, Olive recalled:

> We lived in two Nissen huts with a tortoise coke stove in the middle. The dining
> room and rest room were housed separately in a wooden hut and a wash house
> was also a draughty wooden hut, where water was heated by a coke boiler. The
> toilets were just tin buckets, which we had to empty each night on the midnight
> guard duty. For baths we went to a civilian's house.

There were Barrages everywhere, including Hearsall Common, Spencer Park,
Radford School, Hare & Hounds and the heath in Keresley and Barras Heath. Ray
Holl recalls:

> The balloons nearest to my family in Humber Road were on Gosford Green and
> the corner of Humber Road and London Road. I remember seeing the latter nose
> dive to the ground at the end of its cable and then bounce back, undamaged! This
> resulted in the RAF operatives calling the site 'Hell's Bells Corner!' At one point
> from high ground I counted over 100 barrage balloons over the city!

In May 1940 Anthony Eden appealed for people to join the Local Defence Volunteers,
later the Home Guard; 3,000 Coventry men volunteered in the first week. At one
point over 16,000 served in Coventry's various Home Guard battalions, many
based in factories. Another form of defence, generally forgotten these days, was
Coventry's own Cyclist Battalion. Sid Francis of Walsgrave recalled them:

> When the Local Defence Volunteers were formed I was seventeen years old and
> working at the Humber offices, my boss was Bob Lavell who was just a few
> years older than me and a keen cyclist. The country was very apprehensive over
> the imminent threat of invasion and Bob had this brilliant idea of raising a force
> of young and old cyclists who would patrol the city during the critical period
> from dusk till dawn and link up with each other. This was taken up by the senior

Site 19 Barrage unit as it appeared in 1940; the Co-op, still recognisable today, can be seen on the left.

A Home Guard Unit somewhere in Keresley, Holbrooks, Whitmore Park. They appear to have four rifles, including one held by the youngest member on the bottom right.

officer of the LDV, and the Cyclist Battalion was formed with Bob being CO and general dogsbody. Within a short time we were organised into four sectors that would patrol the perimeter of the city and watch for any paratroopers. The sector that our group had to cover ran from the Grove at the Memorial Park, along the Leamington Road to Stoneleigh, from there to Whitley Aerodrome and along the by-pass to Willenhall, down St James Lane and to the Craven Arms at Binley where we would meet another group covering the Longford/Foleshill sector.

He continues:

Now this took one hour, and we then returned by the same route back to the Grove, and repeated once again, so the duty covered four hours, and was organised from 6 p.m. to 6 a.m., the graveyard shift! We had no equipment other than the LDV armband and we had to pick up a rifle, five rounds of ammo and a tin hat from Queens Road Church, who had a LDV company stationed there. So the rifle, ammo and tin hat were passed to one another when we met up and were duly returned to Queens Road after 6 a.m. Now we cycled in twos and one pair started from the Grove and the other pair from the Craven Arms and we met up on the bypass or Baginton. So there were four cyclists each duty, twelve each night and eighty-four each week and poor Bob had to organise it all! Yes he did, and that ran from June 1940, through the early air raids, the Blitz and the April 1941 raids, until the threat of invasion had passed and when disbanded we went into the regular Home Guard units, and some of the lads were working in factories and others like myself were drafted into the Armed Forces. I think we were the only Cyclist Battalion of the LDV/Home Guard in the country at that time.

Centres were also set up around the city to control all types of defence, such as the Air Defence Control Centre in Radford (Radford Social Club), the main tracking centre under the old Post Office in Hertford Street and the Air Raid Report and Control Centre in St Mary's Street. Maurice Rattigan worked there;

When I was fourteen or fifteen years old I volunteered for the Civil Defence Messenger Service in 1942. I was stationed at an ARP post in Daventry Road and when volunteers were required for duty at the Report and Control Centre I put up my hand. The duty consisted of a full night every eight days. The centre was in the basement of the main police station in the council house building with its entrance in St Mary's Street. Although the Police Station had received a direct hit in April 1941 it had relocated in the same building a few yards down at the next doorway, towards Earl Street. The Report Centre was a room about 20 foot by 12 where about twelve to fifteen Special Constables (in civvies) manned the telephones for incoming air raid incident reports. They filled out duplicated incident reports and us messengers then took these forms across the corridor to the Control Centre where instructions were relayed to the Fire, Ambulance and Rescue Services to attend to the incidents. The Control Centre was about twice the size of the Report Centre and was something similar to an RAF Control Room where the Controller sits above the others dispensing his orders. Our Controller was nominally the Chief Constable, Capt. S. A. Hector, although most times an Inspector took charge. There were maps on the walls highlighting the various incidents.

Part of the defence of the city was of course guns, ack-acks and Bofors. W. R. Copper, an ex NCO in charge of gun maintenance, said,

At the time of the November blitz there were four guns per site around the city. Sites included Keresley (later site of Cardinal Newman School), Binley, Wyken, Tile Hill, Gibbet Hill, Allesley and Ryton. The Royal Artillery Regiment who manned the guns was all male until March 1941; after that women took part too. The three main batteries that were stationed in Coventry until 1943 were 392, 477 and 488. After that date all the 3.7-inch ack-acks were moved to Hastings and Battle to protect London from the flying bomb. These guns were replaced by 4.5 Bofors guns manned by the Home Guard.

Mobile gun crews also moved around the city; I recall my dad saying that before he married, he took Mum home and walked down Beake Avenue (a shorter road then) and nearly jumped out of his skin when a mobile ack-ack opened fire; it wasn't there an hour before! There was also a battery of rocket launchers placed in the Memorial Park in autumn 1941. These rockets, which whooshed into the sky with fiery tails, greatly impressed all who saw them. They may have looked great but were totally ineffective!

Other measures were also taken to protect the city; buildings were painted to camouflage them, shadow factories painted in camouflage paint to blend them into the surrounding fields. Large buildings such as the Hippodrome, a white beacon in the city centre, were painted battleship grey. Cowled oil drums full of petrol and paraffin were placed in certain streets, such as the London Road, and set alight when raids were called, causing a thick black smoke screen. Obstacles were placed on Whitley Common to stop troop gliders landing and pill boxes were set up around the city to defend roads. Soot was scattered along the canal as it came into the city to stop the reflection being used by bombers as a glistening roadway to the city centre on moonlit nights. Black-out regulations came into strict force and at night the streets were black and cars had slits on their headlamps; not surprisingly many people got ran over in the dark! Post boxes, trees, lamps and bollards had white lines painted around them so people wouldn't walk into them. All houses had regulation black-out curtains and most windows were criss-crossed with tape to cut down on shatter blast it they were blown through. The world was full of regulations and it was about to get dangerous, but not yet!

A very rare view of the Police Control Room under the Council House.

Another rare shot showing men manning the phones in the centre.

Opening Events

In September 1939 it was generally believed that gas was the main threat, not necessarily bombs. These notes were issued to the Coventry public:

> All citizens should realise that there is no danger until our anti-aircraft guns have been definitely heard to be firing. This gunfire is unmistakeable as there will be many short sharp loud barks from the guns as opposed to the comparatively rare deep, muffled rumbling of an exploding bomb. Shelter should of course be taken from the danger of splinters of fuses from our own shells when firing starts. Care and attention should be given to your gas mask, they should be kept dry, otherwise they become useless. Every week test your respirator ... A heavy fine will follow any deliberate damage to a respirator. Find out the position of your warden's post, auxiliary fire service and shelters.

It continues:

> Keep your dog or cat in the home at night. If they are found on the streets during an emergency they will probably be destroyed immediately. In an air-raid it is absolutely essential that the streets should be clear to enable the various services to have free passage. Cars should turn into a side street or car park, pedestrians should hasten to the nearest shelter, horses should be tied up. Always keep your bath and buckets full of water. You are then prepared for any fire. Have available a number of air tight containers. In the event of a gas attack your food can be placed in these, to prevent it from becoming contaminated. Other general points to consider are, refrain from crowding, be calm and do not get excited during an air-raid, do not hinder wardens during a raid. ALWAYS CARRY A RESPIRATOR.

Things, however, started to fall from the sky, and they weren't bombs. On the night of 24 May 1940 a Hampden Bomber on a training flight from Tern Hill in Shropshire developed engine trouble. At 11 p.m. as it neared Coventry its engine began to fail and the pilot began circling, dropping flares to try to find somewhere open among the houses to land. Flying at a low height, the bomber struck Site 3 barrage balloon cable based at Charterhouse Fields. The pilot brought the plane down, exploding on the Coventry & North Warwickshire Cricket Ground on the Binley Road. F. E. Hutton, an ex AFS man at Tutton Garage, said of the event, 'We could see the plane was losing height so we set off in pursuit to see if we could give any help. By the time we reached the Coventry Cricket Club, the plane was in the centre of the field well aflame with exploding bullets flying everywhere!' The crew were all killed having bailed out too late; two were killed as they smashed through the roof of the nearby Bulls Head Garage and one was blown clear but killed with only a partially open parachute. The crash was the first major incident dealt with by the newly formed emergency services; their work was often made difficult by the sheer volume of people trying to get a glimpse of the incident. Two of the men were buried in London Road Cemetery and one was returned to his home city of Liverpool. Rumours at the time suggested this was a German observation plane shot down by a Spitfire; wartime bred such rumours!

If this wasn't enough, on 31 May another accident happened. This time Plt Off. J. Crossman, son of Coventry's prospective Labour candidate, R. Crossman, was flying a training aircraft from Ansty Aerodrome when he crashed on the outskirts of the city. He was killed but the other occupant of the plane survived with head injuries. Crossman's father was a city justice and his son was studying at the Bar hoping to follow in his father's footsteps.

A busy Smithford Street in early 1940. A few people are carrying their respirators. Two ARP shelter signs can be seen in the street. The LMS delivery van says, 'Your Courage, Your Cheerfulness, Your Resolution, WILL BRING US VICTORY.'

First Warning

On 25 June 1940 at 12.44 a.m. Coventry had its first real air raid alert. All the services sprung into action, ARP men to their stations and AFS to their fire stations. All waited as searchlights cut into the dark sky looking for the raiders, while ack-ack gunners braced themselves for action! Alan Taylor, who at the time lived in Earlsdon, recalled the event, saying:

> I remember well the night the first sirens sounded in Coventry. There are very few sounds more terrifying, waking you up from a deep sleep. I scrambled out of bed like a mad thing and found it impossible to dress, putting on my trousers backwards. My father did no better as he managed to put two legs down one leg of his long johns. Laughable now but not at all funny at the time ... it was terrifying! We scrambled down to the shelter in the garden and sat there for several hours until the all-clear sounded. Nothing happened ... this would be repeated night after night. We soon learned to listen for the sound of the aircraft before moving.

Mrs Coxwell told me,

> I can recall the sirens sounding for the first time. My father and I went into the garden and saw in the sky, large powerful searchlight beams sweeping across the sky. A plane had got caught in the beams, like a giant silver moth. I will never forget my father's words; he said, ominously, 'They got here then!' I felt fearful of what was to come.

It was a false alarm for Coventry. Bombs, however, were heard in the distance falling in and around the village of Pailton. Three elderly residents were buried in the rubble of their cottage. It was reported, 'They were asleep in their beds when the

Peeping Tom looks from an attic window in Bishop Street, ready for anything!

bomb dropped with terrific impact. Joseph Hill (aged 56) was flung, together with his bed, almost on to the pavement, and his brother and sister were buried inside. Neighbours, one of whom also had his house wrecked, rushed to extricate them.

The report continues:

> Further up the street a flight lieutenant and his wife and baby were in bed when two bombs landed immediately in front of the school opposite. The airman and his wife were flung out of their beds as a piece of bomb shrapnel flew through the window, tore a hole in the bed covering, crashed through the wardrobe and buried itself in the wall. Small splinters pitted the wall around the cot where the baby slept on, uninjured.

The bombs caused a gaping hole in the main school classroom, its roof was blown off and the end of the building demolished. The only actual casualties of the night were twenty chickens in a nearby smallholding; the farmer had literally told his sons to stay away from the windows a split second before they were blown through!

At this time, nearby Ansty Aerodrome still had its flare path lit. Seeing this, the pilot dropped five bombs, taking the corner out of a building! As it droned off on

A bustling Broadgate from the steps of the National Westminster bank; soon all this was gone!

its way the air raid siren was sounded! Apparently this was a common problem at the beginning of the war. It was said that many people slept through this first siren alert, only to be awakened by the 'Raiders Past' siren at 3.13 a.m. and only then took to the shelters. Many were said to be still there when the milkmen were on their rounds!

On 8 August few people in Coventry knew that the King and Queen were among them, visiting Alfred Herbert's, Coventry Gauge and Tool and Civil Defence stations. *The Dundee Courier* of Friday 9 August 1940 reported the event:

The King and Queen yesterday had long talks with men and women working at benches and lathes when they visited two big war factories in Coventry. A deafening welcome was given to them as the engineers hammered their lathes with hammers and spanners. At one of the factories the King and Queen went into a miniature rifle range, and with his first and only shot with the .22 rifle at 25 yards range the King scored a bull's-eye. He persuaded Lord Dudley, Regional Commissioner for the Midlands, who was accompanying him, to try his hand, and Lord Dudley also scored bull at the first attempt. 'Good shooting,' commented the King. Then he turned to the attendant at the range and laughingly asked, 'Can people get nothing but bull's eyes on this range?' 'Only good shots, sir,' was the smiling reply. In a section of one of the works the King and Queen found that a special air-conditioning plant had been installed to maintain a constant temperature. In this building work is carried out with an accuracy of two-millionths of an inch. As a variation of one degree in the temperature makes a difference to the metal of three-millionths of an inch expansion or contraction, according to whether it is warm or cold, it is necessary to keep constant the atmospheric conditions inside the shop. The King tested a measuring gauge which measures up to one-millionth of an inch. Their Majesties frequently stopped for long talks with men and women working at benches and lathes. In one factory they chatted with a workman who had been there fifty years. He handed the King the jeweller's eyeglass which he used for his work, and with it showed him the smallest screw-thread made in the factory. There are 136 threads to every inch. In another department the King and Queen saw youths of fifteen sitting in a classroom being trained for the expert work which they are to do later. In the first factory Their Majesties were particularly impressed to hear that during May, June, and July production exceeded by 50 percent that of the same period last year. Before leaving for London by train the Royal visitors inspected units of Coventry's Civil Defence Services.

Three days later the city mourned the death of one of its most notable and long serving citizens, Colonel Sir William Wyley of Coventry Charterhouse; ex-mayor, ex-everything, Wyley was historically one of the city's greatest characters with lifelong service to the city. Wyley had raised men for the Boer War, the First World War and, if he had survived, he would have done his bit in the Second! Even in death he served the city, leaving his own home, Charterhouse, to be turned into a museum and park for the people of Coventry. His choice for his home, now out of the hands of the council he served so well, only now looks like it may be coming to fruition over 70 years after his death. On the day of his funeral at St Michael's it is said the building was 'packed to its doors'.

On Sunday 18 August 1940 the sirens sounded at 10.53 p.m. and the first actual bombs fell within the boundary of Coventry. A single German aircraft dropped fourteen high explosive bombs on Canley and Cannon Hill roads. The area, which was at that time still under development, received damage to a dozen properties, two being totally demolished. It was reported, 'The most miraculous escape was that of a man and his wife who were sleeping in a house which suffered an almost direct hit, half of the building being blown to bits. Their own room was almost untouched.' After being almost thrown out of bed apparently, the husband went to check what was going on, stepped outside his bedroom door and found himself staring at the stars! The whole of the back and side of the house had been completely blown away leaving their bedroom intact, but with a crack up the wall!

One of the last photographs taken by J. J. Ward before St Michael's was destroyed.

The next door neighbour's house was completely demolished; the occupiers, an army major, his wife and four-year-old daughter, survived because they were away at her mother's. They were shocked on their return, but alive! The next house, despite its proximity to the explosion, survived untouched, and a three-month-old child in its cot slept through the whole incident! Another house seemed to have a large part of the nearby road thrown through their bedroom window onto them while they were in bed. The lady of the house said, 'When you get to my age, you take what is coming to you and are glad it is no worse.'

It was noted at the time the strange unpredictability of bomb blast. 'Windows of houses on either side of a partially demolished property were untouched, yet every inch of glass was blown in some houses that were 30 feet away from an explosion!' One house, which stood ten feet from a crater, was wrecked while the neighbouring property had one window broken and one cracked. It was also noted that, 'There were no craters as such in soft ground, and the secondary, or suction effect, drew back the blown out earth into pyramids like giant sand castles.' The surprising effects of bomb blast would be a regular topic as raids began to intensify; the ability for a bomb to take away half of a building leaving half the rooms untouched, pictures on walls, dinner on the table, was a wonder!

On 20 August 1940 the MDT War Diary records for this night that, 'Soon after midnight enemy planes were heard encircling the city and gun fire was heard in the distance, but was not until three hours later that any bombs were dropped, while warning sirens did not sound until 3.45 a.m.' This was followed by the first screamer bombs, that is bombs with screamer devices in their noses; the noise was meant to instil terror into those who heard it. Little damage was done as these screamers fell north of the city on open ground, damaging the LMS railway line from Coventry to Birmingham. Other bombs were dropped close to the Standard factory and Coventry Gauge and Tool. It was noted that that night a heavy barrage was put up which left the city streets littered with shrapnel. Dad once told me that falling shrapnel sounded like heavy rain!

Philip Deeming recalled the event for a different reason:

> We had several air raid warnings but nothing ever happened. I was spending the evening at the Gaumont Cinema with my girlfriend (later my wife). The sirens had gone and on leaving the cinema we realised something was different. Searchlights were lighting the sky and it seemed very ominous. Hurrying along the Binley Road we heard our first bombs dropping, so we ran into a wooden garage that was open near Stoke Green. Crouching on the floor my girlfriend laddered her stockings – this was the tragedy of the evening as they were on coupons!

The previous day and night the city had received three separate siren alerts, and a number of bombs dropped, giving it a night of broken sleep. On 25 August the sirens wailed at 9.47 in the late evening. Patrons of the Rex Cinema, Coventry's newest premier cinema, left and headed home in the black-out. Over several hours five waves of raiders passed over, caught in intense searchlight beams and watched by many as shells burst around them from ack-ack and Bofors guns. Incendiaries were dropped and it was said at the time that AFS men who tried to deal with them were machine gunned by fighter bombers. Although many bombs were dropped there were no casualties and few injuries.

The Rex Cinema, famously scheduled to be playing *Gone with the Wind* the following day, was hit by an HE bomb which crashed through the roof of the auditorium blasting the area apart and bringing down the roof. No one was in the

Bomb damage in Well Street, 25 August.

building. One of the few things to survive was the safe, which still contained Sunday night's takings. It was noted that,

> A dozen birds, some of them tropical, sat on their perches in the cafe above the vestibule of the wrecked cinema today. The glass of their aviary had been blown away, but the birds had ignored their chance to escape. Adjacent shops had most of their windows completely blown out.

A delayed action bomb blew nearby, by houses, creating a crater 15 feet deep and 30 feet across, which quickly filled with water from a smashed mains. 'About a dozen large pieces of roadway were hurled through the roofs of two lock up shops ... and they were demolished.' Several house received blast damage one witness said,

> The bomb made a thunderous noise, the vibration rolled us about the shelter, and we could hear bricks and rubble raining down and bouncing on the shelter roof.

Further damage was done in the area including Kenning & Son in West Orchard and Baddeley & Co. in Lower Ford Street, which was burnt out. There was one injury that night; a man passing the Rex had three pieces of plate glass embedded in his buttock. Apparently, when they were removed, he was given them as souvenirs!

On the night of 26/27 August bombs caused damage to the Daimler No. 1 factory in Radford and garages by Gosford Green, and the Goods Yard received a small number of hits. The following night (28 August) thirteen bombs were dropped in the Hillfields area causing the first actual fatalities of the war in Coventry; sixteen were killed and forty injured, mainly in the Cambridge Street area. On 28 August another small raid damaged twenty-one buses at the Transport Garage. Brett's Stamping in Harnall Lane was hit and the Ordnance Works in Red Lane received a number of hits, destroying an air raid shelter and smashing up gun mountings, torpedo tubes and leaving a 30-foot crater, 4 inches deep in a concrete floor!

An interesting photograph taken on 26 August showing bomb damage in Well Street and in the background stands the Rex with its windows blown out from internal blast.

Wallace Road, Stephenson Road Incident

On the night of Monday 16 September 1940 enemy planes passed over Coventry on three occasions. The MDT reported that, 'It is believed that one of the bombs was an aerial torpedo, which struck the roadway and was deflected into a block of houses.' One resident said:

> I could see the engines turning over and I thought it was a British plane, until suddenly the pilot opened fire with machine guns, I dived into the house and as I closed the door the bombs exploded, straddling my house. It seemed that the bombs were right outside the door, for the house rocked and all the windows were blown in ... People in other houses were in bed and were blown onto the floor.

An off duty AFS man said that he saw the plane make a 'pot hook' turn and heard the sound of machine gun fire. He dashed into his house as his door was violently blown in on top of him. As he fell he accidently pushed his wife onto the stove, which with a second explosion jumped three inches into the air. Apparently the contents of one large bomb crater ended up on top of a house. The MDT mentions that some were killed, but only mentions the actual deaths of two white rabbits, killed by concussion.

Of the event, Roy Clarke recalled these details:

> The night the German plane clipped the wire brought utter chaos to the top end of Stevenson Road, which lies at the back of Wallace Road. The one bomb burst the gas main where it bounced first, right outside No. 40. It went on to demolish a whole row of four houses. I believe it killed all the occupants except two; the man at No. 58, I think his name was Bob, stepped outside and lost both his legs, but lived, and so did his daughter Marjorie. It is said they both died on a later raid on Coventry.

Roy continued, 'The four houses demolished were Nos 58, 60, 62 and 64, and the others either side were badly damaged, but repaired after the war. I lived at No. 54 and our entire block was wrecked and we had to move out.'

Of the night, Roy remembered,

My mother, sister, twelve month old baby brother and myself were buried in the Anderson shelter in the garden, until they moved the rubble. I remember the baby crying loudly and when we heard the plane my mother shouted: 'Shut him up, the Germans will hear him.'

The blast from the door pushed the door of the shelter in, hitting my sister over the head, knocking her out, and out went the candle with it. It was like being in a vacuum for a moment, even the baby stopped crying for a few seconds, then started again. It was pitch black and seemed like forever until the rescue people came. It was frightening, my mother shouting, 'Oh my God!' and the baby screaming. My sister was out cold and we couldn't find the matches to light the candle.

When the rescue party finally reached them, Roy recalls,

The first we knew was when someone made a small hole in the rubble to shine a torch through. A voice shouted, 'Are you alright, do you want anything?' Mother

An extremely rare photograph of bomb damage in Wallace Road. Two houses appear to have gone!

replied, 'Yes, a cigarette please.' An arm came through the hole with some loose cigarettes. 'How about a match?' mother shouted, and the arm obliged; meanwhile my sister was still unconscious!

When we climbed out it was like a scene from hell, everything was gone, houses, sheds, fences, line posts. In the road was a huge gushing flame from the smashed gas main. The noise along with the men shouting made it a scene no-one could ever forget. The saddest part was the stretchers with the dead, covered in dust and dirt. The lady from next door, but one was on the first stretcher, the tiny baby on her chest. She still had her arms around it.

In nearby Wallace Road he recalls, 'The Anderson in Wallace Road a few feet from ours had a direct hit. I believe the man and wife disappeared and the body of a younger man was blown two to three hundred yards down to the allotments.' Roy concludes,

The story was that the plane was looking for the Daimler works, and it seemed to come from that direction to us. The engines were throbbing so we knew it had a heavy load of bombs. Minutes later it came roaring back releasing its load. We were told later that it caught the balloon wire at Keresley, by the Shepherd & Shepherdess, which spun it around and damaged it.

Another rare shot taken in the winter showing damage to Wallace Road taken from Hardy Road.

Maurice Burnell with his father and sister standing by the barrage balloon at Site 19.

The male crew of Site 19 in August 1940.

Roy believed that when the plane crashed one of the crew was taken to the Gas Yard in Hill Street, which was used as a mortuary to show him what he had done. 'My father worked there, this was early in the war and the people were shocked.'

Bob Beaufoy's parents lived at No. 70 Stevenson Road at that time with their young daughter. Bob was born later, but he recalls the story passed down to him of the night in question:

They heard the sound of the approaching aircraft, very low and seemingly in trouble and rushed out into the back garden to see it. As it passed overhead bombs could be seen falling and Dad shouted, 'Lie down' but Mum was too afraid and just crouched against the wall. It was just as well for a kerbstone landed where she would have lain, and I wouldn't be telling you this! Remembering their four year old daughter Sheila was upstairs in bed, Dad had to climb over the front door, which had been blown onto the stairs, to find her still asleep, but covered in plaster from the ceiling. Being partially disabled from a football injury he couldn't get back down and had to await rescue. Later he found an Anderson shelter in the entry at the rear which had been blown from a nearby garden. The family inside appeared to be uninjured, but were all dead!

Others who were killed that night in Wallace Road were the family of the town crier, Stan Bacon. Stan was a young boy when the incident happened but never forgot that terrible night when his entire family were wiped out by a direct hit on their Anderson in the back garden. Many houses over the area were damaged including Hammersley's the grocer and Caswell the chemist in Wallace Road.

There is much controversy over which barrage balloon cable struck this aircraft. It appears that although generally Site 19's barrage by the Shepherd & Shepherdess seems to have caused it, others claim it was another balloon, such as one on Gosford Green, or the one behind the Hare & Hounds in Keresley.

Maurice Burnell, who still lives by Site 19, said,

On Monday night, September 16, there had been an air raid and the all clear had sounded shortly before midnight. We came out of the air raid shelter and I was standing in the garden with my father and my sister Dorothy when we heard the sound of low flying aircraft coming from the north-west. It sounded like a fighter plane, as we could hear only one engine. In seconds it went all quiet, but not for long, as we heard it approaching again from the same direction. What we did not know was that the balloon cable on site 19 had clipped the starboard wing of the plane. Seconds later there were massive explosions as the plane jettisoned its bombs. It wasn't until the next morning that we found that the bombs had fallen on Wallace Road as the people were coming out of the air raid shelters, and men, women and children were killed.

J. C. Mason of Bedworth told me about the same event in 2003; he said,

> On that night the sirens had sounded early and my parents and I had gone into our Anderson shelter where we lived in Butlin Road, near Hen Lane. These shelters were always cold and damp, so when the all-clear sounded we dashed back to the house for a cup of tea and to try and get back to sleep. All was quiet, the raid had passed, and then I heard the sound of an aircraft re-starting its engines. Rushing to the front door I clearly against the moonlit sky saw a Heinkel III bomber.
>
> It was low down flying towards Coventry from Bedworth, with sparks showering from the rooftops [see following MDT report regarding shafts of sparks]. I found later that these were caused by a balloon cable embedded into its wing, striking the roofs, bringing it down. I shouted to my father, 'It's a Heinkel bomber,' and he shouted back, 'Don't be daft the all-clear's gone.' This was followed by massive explosions; the Heinkel had ditched its bombs.

Apparently, that Christmas, his father met two of the balloon crew from behind the Hare & Hounds in Watery Lane, Keresley, and he invited them to Christmas dinner. John said the men claimed that it was their barrage which struck the bomber and they had something to prove it!

> They had two trophies off the bomber, a propeller and part of the rudder, and these they took me to see on Boxing Day. They gave me a diffused incendiary bomb with Nazi insignia on it as a memento. Shortly after, they were gone to strengthen the defences of London. We never heard of them again.

Both the MDT and the diary of Mary Blomefield, recorded that the plane came down in fields between Walsgrave and Withybrook, and the crew bailed out. The MDT states that:

> Skimming hedges, with flames pouring from the fuselage, the Junkers 88 [not a Heinkel this time] crashed with a tremendous explosion near a village. Home Guard and military rushed in the spot but were unable to rescue two German airmen from the wreckage. Meanwhile two other members of the crew had taken to their parachutes and were captured.

The farmer whose land it crashed on was certain that a British fighter was on its tail before it dived in flames, leaving hundreds of pieces of wreckage over three fields. The crashed bomber was described as being like a ball of fire with shafts of sparks shooting from it, the glow lit up the neighbourhood and the fields echoed with exploding ammunition.

One report states that three aircrew were killed as their chutes failed to open and the surviving member broke his ankle on landing. Another report states that two bailed out, one breaking his leg and the other his ankle. This is backed up by a later report as more than one appears to have survived and was taken to the Coventry and Warwickshire Hospital for treatment. These airmen were still in the hospital on 21 November as the Minister of Health called for a report to be made on their 'reception and treatment'. Captain Strickland, a Conservative councillor assured the minister that the 'German airmen were accommodated in single bedded wards and that they may not be seen by other people'. He added that, 'The hospital authorities appear to have acted quite properly in the matter.'

It appears that on the night in question three barrage balloons were lost; the Site 19 balloon came down in Broadgate. It is entirely possible that the plane, claimed by the *Midland Daily Telegraph* to be a Junkers 88, hit more than one cable that night before bringing devastation down on some Keresley homes. I'll leave the last word to the German pilot to add to the confusion; he actually claimed that he dropped the bombs before he hit the barrage balloon! Throughout the rest of September there were numerous air warnings and bombers flying over the city but no more bombs dropped.

Possibly the only surviving picture of the bomber at the crash site.

The October Raids

There were over fifty siren alerts from the 1st of the month, but it was Saturday 12 October which was said to be the start of the 'local *blitzkrieg*.' This raid, quickly followed by a second raid on Monday, were two of the first heavy raids of Coventry's war. The raid started just after 8.30 a.m. when incendiary bombs were dropped on the LMS goods yard in Warwick Road. More bombs fell on Warwick Road, Queens Road, Bishop Street and Leicester Row. Pool Meadow Car Park was hit and twenty-two corporation buses were damaged. The raid continued for two hours with waves of aircraft dropping their devastating loads from a great height on the blacked-out city, which was brightly lit by a beautiful full hunter's moon.

The MDT war diary says,

Central area suffered spectacular damage. A HE scored a direct hit on the City Arcade (on Messrs. Adams, china stores), and every shop front in the arcade were wrecked. Fire station tower was badly damaged by a bomb which exploded on the roof of the drill yard, and new Hippodrome had a fortunate escape when bomb fell on Matterson's next door. A serious fire was caused by an oil type bomb at Waters Garage and wine stores.

It continues,

Large numbers of incendiaries fell in and around the central thoroughfare, including two on the roof of the council house and two more in the cathedral church yard. The most spectacular fires were at the Swift Skating Rink (unlucky place this - previous fire and damage by the IRA's explosion) and Coventry Motor Mart, London Road. Both were gutted despite intensive work by fire services ... Motor Mart was a terrific blaze, at least one petrol tank having exploded ...

The already badly wrecked Rex Cinema in Corporation Street received a second hit and damage was done to surrounding properties such as Hogarth Shoes, Foleshill Road, which got hit by a number of HEs. Devastation spread over into many areas including Hillfields and the Walsgrave Road. It was reported that 75 per cent of the Tungsten Carbide factory in Stoney Stanton Road was flattened. On this night 217 incidents were dealt with by the services.

The Revd Clitheroe of Holy Trinity, in his excellent memoir *Coventry under Fire*, says of the night,

> The sirens sounded night after night. One night the alert came early in the evening and my eldest son Donald and I were on our way to the church [fire watching] when an alarming incident occurred. Bombs were falling on the town, and we had just passed the Crane's Hotel at the top of Bishop Street, and said goodnight to two police officers on duty there, when the scream of bombs caused us to take such cover as we could in the shop fronts. When the explosions had ceased a cloud of

A bomb crater in the city centre, 13 October.

dust hung over the road, the Crane's had gone, and the policemen (Sergeant Fox and PC Leadham) had been killed.

He continues, 'We reached the church quickly as possible and remained on duty all that night. I asked Donald of what he thought whilst the bombs were falling, "Only," he said, "whether the next one would hit us!" We escaped by the comfortable margin of at least sixty yards. But the deaths of those fine policemen saddened us.'

It seems that, previously to their deaths, the officers had witnessed a bomb falling which hadn't detonated. In response, they had evacuated the Crane's and were clearing the area to get the public to safety when they were killed. Half of the Crane's Hotel was destroyed. Also that night two ARP wardens, J. H. Phillips and D. J. Williams, were killed when a time bomb exploded in Stamford Avenue near the Leamington Road. Sixteen factories were hit including the GEC and the Triumph but no major damage except a large fire in the Daimler No. 1 Aircraft Factory in Radford and an oil bomb at Waters Garage and Wine Store.

Bombs also hit Matterson's and the Fire Station and incendiaries fell in St Michael's churchyard. The Swift Skating Rink was completely destroyed by fire, after surviving a previous fire! The Rex Cinema received another hit and nearby buildings were damaged. A street shelter in Aldbourne Road, Radford, took a direct

A policeman checks bomb damage while men clear up in a city centre street on 13 October.

hit killing the seven people inside. Damage was spread from Radford to Walsgrave. Buses were damaged and tram lines blown up. Thirty one people were killed.

The city had hardly settled before it all started again. There were two warnings on Monday 14 October at 7.15 to 7.41 p.m. and 8.08 to 1.34 a.m., although the actual raid took place during the second warning. Betty Hardy told me in 2001:

My fourteen year old brother was sent to the shelter to save a place for my mother and me at about 7 o'clock, it was a moonlit night. Mother was doing the washing in the gas boiler and while that was boiling she wrote a birthday card for my sister and decided to call on the lady next door for a stamp. As she opened the back door so did the neighbour, the light shone out and I heard a single plane overhead. I shouted shut that door, and then the warden shouted, 'Turn that bloody light out.'

I shouted to my mother, 'Come in quick. It's a Jerry plane!' Then as she came in it dropped a bomb and we were trapped under rubble. It was a semi-detached house in Lythalls Lane and a big timber of wood fell and trapped my mother. At the other end in the house, Mr Warren was killed. We finally got out, but mother and I ran up the road to Mrs Lutterworth's who was a friend. She took us in and gave us a drink of tea, then took us both to the dog stadium where the shelter was to join my brother.

The next morning we returned to what was left of our house. There was just the front shell left and a policeman on guard. There were soldiers searching for the bodies of me and my mother, they wouldn't let us in. Mother said, 'It's my house, what's left of it.' He replied, 'I'm sorry but the gentleman next door was killed outright, and the soldiers are looking for bodies of a mother and daughter.' We had to get Mrs Dodd to tell them who we were. The reports in the paper said it was an aerial torpedo that hit our house.

Diane Wagstaff recalled that her father, a fire officer in the city, was having a busy time:

While Dad was on duty, which seemed to be every night, Mum, Ron, Auntie and I went down into the Anderson shelter in our garden. The sirens always seemed to sound as auntie started to wash her hair, and not having a bathroom we would take bowls of water to the shelter for her to finish. Sometimes we were in the shelter for many hours, after school until the next morning. Mum and auntie, who must have been so worried and anxious about Dad and uncle who was a soldier, made it fun. We played cards, Ludo, I spy, sang, played with our toys and auntie told us stories, which were sometimes scary. They would take it in turns to go to the house when it quietened down to make a meal. I remember lovely stews, rabbit, oxtail or just veg. If we had no meat every scrap was mopped up with bread. I've not mentioned Gran; she was a character, she refused to go down the shelter. Instead she had an armchair under the stairs in what we called the bogey hole. She had a bottle of Guinness, a plate of sandwiches and a tin hat and she was quite content! However on a particularly bad night auntie persuaded her to go down to the Anderson, she tripped and fell into the rose bush, she had cuts all over her. She never went down again!

As things got worse, Diane's father's work load grew and decided it would be best to move his wife, Diane and her brother Ron to the relative safety of Princethorpe. Diane recalled that, 'When it was dark, if you stood on the hill by the abbey you could see the glow of the fires in Coventry, and then we would say a little prayer for Dad.'

The new Owen Owen department store was hit by a single large bomb, which crashed through three floors and exploded against a massive girder, doing major damage. The store, however, reopened in four days. A fire bomb burned through into the inner roof of the Cathedral causing extensive damage, its first actual hit, but was quickly dealt with. The opera house suffered a major fire and the fire station was hit again and the Rex was hit for the third time. Incidents were reported over large areas of the city and ten factories received minor damage.

Ford's Hospital showing the main blast area from the rear left. Amazingly on that side the lower courses of large sandstones are blasted out and yet the ancient timbers and wattle and daub withstood the force.

Perhaps the most shocking incident of these raids was, however, the strike on Ford's Hospital, Coventry's oldest almshouse, home to a small group of old ladies. The bomb was said to have fallen towards the back of the fifteenth-century building. The ancient oak and teak frontage was blown outwards, but held, and the lower stonework was blown out! None of the occupants were in the shelter, nine survived, one clutching a bottle of brandy! Eight were killed and six seriously injured. Much of the building was later restored by local historian and builder Abe Jephcott, and remains one of the finest almshouses in England. This raid covered a wide area from Hillfields to Old Church Road in Foleshill and it was noted heavier calibre bombs were being used and many larger fires. Fifty-three people were killed, 200 injured and forty homes totally destroyed.

On 16 October twenty-six-year-old airman Squadron Leader J. A. Davies crashed his Hurricane fighter in a field in Whitley after clipping his starboard wing on the cable of a barrage balloon (Site 9), shortly after 2 p.m. at Cheylesmore, while leading three Hurricanes (308 Polish Squadron, Baginton) at 1,000 feet. The Hurricane struck the ground and burst into flames killing the pilot, while machine gun bullets exploded and fire withheld those trying to rescue the unfortunate flyer. There were Hurricanes based at Baginton and a couple for a short time at the old Radford Aerodrome. Of the event Maurice Rattigan, who was thirteen at the time, recalled:

I came home from school to find an RAF Hurricane fighter crashed on open land about 120 yards away from the rear of our house in Shortley Road. Once again a balloon cable had been responsible, but this time it was the one sited on the corner of Humber Road and London Road ... I visited the site and people were picking up souvenirs. There were plenty of bits of the plane about, and bullets, and I picked up part of the pilot's charred parachute harness, and over 55 years later passed it on to the Midland Air Museum at Baginton.

On Friday 18 October the Royal Engineers' bomb disposal squad removed a 560lb bomb from the previous raid, which had buried itself in the ground in Chapel Street, near West Orchard Chapel. The bomb was loaded on a lorry and taken to Whitley Common to be detonated. During the unloading operation the bomb exploded; Second Lieutenant Campbell and seven of his men were killed. An eighth man at a distance received a head wound but survived. The bomb disposal squad stationed in Quinton Road were well liked in the city, not only for their heroism but their general character.

Martyn Hammond recalled:

One day in school (Folly Lane) we heard a large explosion, which we know to be the delayed bomb being set off on Whitley Common. We gathered from local talk that soldiers were about to lift it off a lorry when it detonated. After school a group of us went to Whitley Common and walked around the area. It was a

UXB men in Coventry; not the crew who were killed but a team serving the city in 1941. UXBs were notoriously unstable, this was one of the most dangerous occupation on the Home Front. These are brave fellows!

gruesome scene with bits of men hanging from the trees and bushes, with parts of their uniforms and the lorry strewn all over. We were surprised that the area wasn't cordoned off and us children allowed to wander around. My brother picked up a piece of a soldiers web belt and brought it home.

Maurice Rattigan, then also a child, arrived at the site of the explosion. He recalled, 'Policemen were picking pieces up and putting them in sacks. My friend found half of a ten shilling note!' This was normal; all wartime boys feverently collected souvenirs. These fearless UXB men were buried together in the London Road Cemetery and two posthumously received the George Medal.

On Saturday 19 October at noon a hit and run raider came into the city flying low and dodging the barrage balloon cables. It machine gunned the workers as they were leaving the Standard factory and dropped a number of small bombs around the Birchfield Road area fracturing a gas main. It also machine gunned an AFS station which had previously received two hits. A local estate agent was machine gunned as he drove down Dulverton Avenue, a bullet struck the back of his car and caused damage underneath. Bill Tisdale, an FAP attendant in the area, also recalled the event:

> During an alert I was outside with an ambulance driver, Mrs Adams. We spotted a plane in the direction of Tile Hill, there were puffs of smoke then the plane banked. Mrs. Adams said, 'Oh look he's coming towards us.' I pulled her behind the wall of sandbags just as he opened fire; the bullets struck the ground and the houses on the opposite side of the road. There were red crosses on top of the ambulances in plain view but that didn't deter him from opening fire.

Alan Savage recalled:

> I remember the Dornier bomber, I was working at the Standard Service Department opposite the cinema at the time. The plane was seen in the area of the railway line. The Home Guard had had a machine gun mounted on the roof of the service department. The old stalwarts were designated to man it, but they got up to the gun and realised they had no ammo. I believe they were awaiting ammo and tuition on the gun. If they had had the ammo it was an easy target! I believe they went through the motions. It was a big joke at the time and it was reported that the plane reached base! Quite a few went outside to view the scene. The plane was really low and what a target if they had the ammo! The bomber also flew across Hearsall Common machine gunning people, and for many years afterwards glass in the telephone box there had a line of bullet holes through it! A report in the press stated that it was a daylight raid on the paint shop of the Standard Motor Company undertaken by a Flying Officer Storp. It also quoted him as a very brave man to manoeuvre between the barrage balloons.'

It didn't, of course, mention the fact that he was machine gunning civilians, but that happened a number of times in Coventry! The air raid sirens sounded fifteen minutes after the attack.

Later at 7.43 the sirens sounded again and bombers began unloading incendiaries and HEs regularly until 10.13. The area of damage was from the city centre spreading to the north of the city. The worst incident of the night happened in Castle Street when a house took a direct hit and collapsed into the cellar, crushing to death the fifteen people sheltering there. Seven others were killed when their Anderson was hit in Hen Lane, Holbrooks.

Various small raids, mainly aimed at factories but of course wrecking civilian lives, continued over October. On the 19th the Riley, the Humber Hillman, Ordnance Works, GEC, Armstrong Siddeley, City Plating and Brett's Stamping were all hit; also St Peter's Mission hall in Sackville Street was hit. Johnson & Mason, a firm set up in the nineteenth century, had its mineral water factory destroyed in Vine Street.

The FAP team in Coundon. Bill Tisdale is the first man of the back row (right).

St Paul's in Foleshill Road amid the smoke of a night's bombing.

On 20 October Armstrong Siddeley, Coventry Motor Fittings and Morris Motors were hit, as was the Globe Cinema and the Regal. Also St Peter's Church in Foleshill received damage to the roof, while Foleshill Baptist Church in Broad Street was partially destroyed by fire bombs. The Central Hall was damaged on 21 October and Foleshill Congregational Church had a single bomb fall into the graveyard leaving a huge crater, smashing gravestones and damaging the church roof. Singer Motors in Canterbury Street received extensive damage as did Courtaulds on the Foleshill Road, although this affected output very little. Some pupils cheered as Radford School was seriously damaged! Two hundred dogs were put down by the RSPCA as owners could not deal with them under the circumstances, or they were evacuated. Many owners kept their best pals, but being unable to take them into public shelters, had to stay home with them during raids. A local terrier at the time was noted for standing over a baby's crib to protect the child during raids! My Dad met a very large nervous dog walking by Radford Church during one particularly

A relaxed AFS crew photographed by James Armer in Stoney Stanton Road in 1940.

heavy raid; he took the dog home. It stayed for a while, then during another raid bolted and was never seen again!

On 22 October Rotherham's in Spon Street was hit, as was BTH in Ford Street; the works received much damage and several air raid shelters were destroyed. The Sibree Hall was partially demolished and Holy Trinity received damage to the roof and smashed stain glass windows. All Saints in Vecquary Street had considerable damage to the roof and windows. Also St Mary's Hall in Bayley Lane, Britain's best medieval guildhall, received a single hit from a high explosive bomb; this damaged woodwork and windows in the armoury, kitchen and Old Council Chamber, where burned wood can still be seen, and in the Princes Chamber, a chip in the Jacobean Fireplace. More significantly, Caesar's Tower at the rear of the hall was blown up within six feet of the ground. This was probably the oldest standing structure in Coventry, believed to be a relic of Coventry Castle, dating to the twelfth century. The tower was later rebuilt, almost, but not quite, to its original form.

On 26 October the Alfred Herbert works was hit and the following night Maudslay Aero Engines in Parkside were hit; also the Humber works received considerable damage. Bell Green Congregational church was damaged and the Aylesford Inn in Aylesford Street was totally destroyed. On the night of the 29/30th St Lawrence's Foleshill had the roof of the nave and the south aisle totally destroyed, floor and pews also received considerable damage and the vicarage was also damaged. On all these nights numerous homes and other properties were also damaged.

November Raids up to Moonlight
1–13 November 1940

On the morning of 1 November a single raider flew over the city, dropping a string of bombs over Silver Street, resulting in twelve deaths and major damage. W. Lants in Bond Street, mineral water makers since the nineteenth century, was partly demolished, much of its stock was lost and two lorries were blown up. This long established company never recovered. Also the Midland Confectioners and Matterson & Huxley in Hales Street received significant damage. Stoke Bowling club also took minor damage as did the Armstrong Siddeley Sports Club and the Chace Hotel on the London Road. 2 November onwards saw a break in the fine weather with heavy rain bringing some much needed peace to the city. It was however noted that the lone bomber had also dropped two large DAs which caused chaos after their discovery with the blocking of Warwick Road and Smithford Street. Despite the lull there were siren alerts in the city every night leading up to 14 November.

On Monday 4 November Coventry police officers all added this entry into their notebooks:

At midday 3 November 1940 a complete enemy parachute, complete with harness and overalls and flying helmet, was found neatly folded and placed in hedge by side of footpath in Haverham [about 60 miles away]. The parachute was wet but the clothing inside was dry and appears it may have dropped down during the last day or two. A packet of food inside had recently been opened and consumed. The parachute has without doubt been used by an enemy parachutist who is still at large. There is no trace of a crashed aircraft and the parachutist was undoubtedly deliberately dropped, special enquiries to be made...

The enemy parachutist, a favourite cliché of wartime films, was for real!

On that same night the police in Coventry had other things to contend with, when enemy raiders dropped bombs in Whitley, damaging houses and hitting the Corporation Greenhouses in Shortly Road, smashing glass and causing minor building damage. Also the London Road Pumping Station received a direct hit. Over in Foleshill more houses were damaged and the Congregational church received extensive damage, its roof and walls were blown out and 50 feet of flagged paving destroyed by an HE. Foleshill was revisited on 7 November when Ye Olde Hall in Lythalls Lane was hit. Raiders were back on the same night and 12 November.

A significant event happened on Saturday 9 November, but not in Coventry – in Germany. Hitler and other Nazi leaders were in Munich celebrating the 1923 founding of the Nazi Party. To Hitler's annoyance, when he was about to give a speech the event was interrupted for two hours by an RAF raid. Hitler's speech broadcast was cancelled and a stick of bombs hit the beer hall where the founding event took place. This event later was to play a part in 14 November.

On 13 November the Duchess of Gloucester visited Coventry. She took lunch with the Mayor in the Council House before touring the city by car and by foot, despite the fact that the streets were heavy with wet clay from the many craters. The Duchess stopped frequently to talk to people. An elderly lady called Mrs Arnold particularly took her interest. She was apparently famous in her little patch for refusing to leave her home despite the fact that all her neighbours' houses had been destroyed, leaving her isolated. 'But why should I leave?' she said, 'I have no-where to go, but in any case we have to win the war, and I think it is up to the older ones to show the younger people we are not frightened.' Mrs Arnold told the Duchess that when the first bomb fell she was nearly blown off her couch and only two doors away the man and his wife had died by gas poisoning from a broken pipe. The Duchess continued her walk, clambering over the smashed bricks and mud which covered everything, while bystanders waved and clapped her. Walking in a side street the duchess passed a woman wiping her mud splattered windows. 'It must be difficult to make those windows look smart,' she said, to which the woman, continuing in her work, replied, 'We shall try anyway!'

Then the party arrived in Silver Street, and standing before smashed down homes the Chief Inspector described what happened and that twelve people had lost their lives. The Duchess was introduced to Mr and Mrs Oldfield in an adjoining house. Of the twelve killed, seven were relatives of Mr Oldfield, including his mother, brothers, sisters and a niece, whose banns of marriage were to have been published the day after the bombing. Mr Oldfield explained how he had been trapped by heavy timbers for an hour and a half before he was dug out. 'I lost seven of my own people ... but still it is war,' he said. The Duchess then went to visit the injured from the November raids in the Coventry and Warwickshire Hospital. Here, much to her surprise and pleasure, she was cheered in the men's ward. She talked to many, particularly to a Mr Howard who had a fractured spine after spending seven hours

Women salvaging belongings in the huddled old central street in Coventry.

buried under rubble in a hotel. In the next ward she met a mother and daughter, who had been injured when their street shelter took a hit from an HE. After dispensing much sympathy and cheer around the city, the Duchess left in her car, cheered by passersby. Her visit was the main story in the MDT on the following day. Also for the first time it was reported that Caesar's Tower at the rear of St Mary's Hall had been almost entirely destroyed. The building, thought to be the oldest standing structure in Coventry, it was hoped would be restored ... the date of publishing ... 14 November 1940.

Moonlight Sonata

Ronald Lewin, who has studied the Enigma messages, states in his book *Ultra Goes To War* that:

> Coventry, the ancient city of three spires, has been twice crucified: once by the German air force and once by those who have spread a legend that the slaughter of its citizens during the raid of 14 November 1940 was a sacrifice – a sacrifice because the raid was known about through Ultra many hours or even days in advance, yet no warning was given to the cities authorities, or to those responsible for its defence, for fear of compromising Ultra's precious secret. Since this allegation is totally untrue, it mocks those who died or suffered.

Amazingly, many now believe Churchill sacrificed the city, a theme perpetuated by newspaper articles, blogs and plays such as Alan Pollock's *One Night in November*. Some now even believe that the people knew about this during wartime! In reality this story first appeared in the 1970s and has since many times been proven wrong. The idea that the RAF were held back and Coventry sacrificed by Churchill to protect Enigma is known by all serious historians to be nonsense! This nonsense carries itself along by people adding minor unproven additions to the story, most of unknown origin, which help perpetuate the myth. The reason for this appears to be that some just like a good conspiracy and others simply dislike Churchill!

Back in 1940, the German Luftwaffe normally raided during daylight, then it was noticed later that year that a specialist squadron, Kesselring's *Kampfgruppe* 100 or KGr. 100, consisting of about thirty Heinkel 111 bombers, were behaving differently. In October the group began to regularly use the new X-Gerät radio beaming system to take them to night time targets. Acting as pathfinders, KGr 100 would drop flares which hung in the sky, then incendiaries to start fires to mark the target for the groups that followed. Churchill was told at the time that they appeared to be practising! Churchill was kept informed but he was never first to know, this usually came eventually to him via Air Force intelligence. On 6 November one of KGr. 100 was shot down and the X-Gerät receiver came into our hands, but sadly because the army and RAF were arguing over who was responsible for the wreckage it sat for days on a beach, and the intelligence which could have been gained from the machine was delayed. This meant that the audio frequency settings weren't released until 27 November, so they couldn't be used to jam the signal on 14 November.

On 11 November, the Intelligence Branch of the Air Ministry received an Ultra decrypt of an Enigma message sent on 9 November from KGr. 100's HQ at Vannes, stating, 'Prepare for new targets as follows ... New Targets 51, 52 and 53' (these were numbers allocated to actual targets).' It was noted that instructions to set the X-Gerät beam were to the minute and not to the usual second. This minor lack of accuracy implied that they planned to use the new system of fire laying a target developed by KGr. 100. The codename 'Korn' also appeared but at that time meant nothing.

On the same day a German pilot who was shot down on the 9th told his cell mate that riots had broken out in London and Buckingham Palace had been stormed and Goring now believed it was the time for a psychologically shattering raid between 15 November and 20 November. It was to happen when there was a full moon and Coventry and Birmingham would be the targets and every bomber in the German air force would take part. The main targets, he stated, would be the 'workmen's dwellings ... in order to undermine the working classes who are believed to be so near revolt'. This information was sent to the Director of Air Intelligence on the following day with additional information that the raid was code named Moonlight Sonata (*Mondscheinsonate*) and was probably a three phase attack. The officer also stated that, 'I thought it well to bring this information to your notice although on account of the source it should be treated with reserve, as he [the pilot] is yet untried.' He added,

I believe that S/L Humphreys [Senior Intelligence Liaison Officer at Bletchley] has pretty definite information that the attack is to be against London and the Home Counties and he believes that it is in retaliation for Munich. The objective (Coventry and Birmingham) should also be regarded as doubtful as probably his information is later.

On 12 November air staff gave a memorandum to the Directorate of Home Operations based on the 9 November decryption. It made certain points about what it believed was to happen:

The codename of the upcoming operation is Moonlight Sonata.
It is likely this raid will occur between 15 November (full moon) and 20 November.

It will likely be a night operation.

Air fleet 2 and 3 and KGr 100 will be participating.

The following target areas are mentioned:

Target 1: It is uncertain where this area lies. It is possibly central London.

Target 2: Greater London and the circle Windsor-St. Albans-Epping-Gravesend-Westerham.

Target 3: The triangle bounded by lines connecting Farnborough Aerodrome-Reading-Maidenhead.

Target 4: The district Faversham-Rochester-Sheerness.

These target areas were not from Enigma but a captured German map and the raid dates originate from the German pilot. This is all that was officially known about Moonlight Sonata at this point. On that same day Air Staff organised a counter offensive called Operation Coldwater. This would consist of jamming radio beams, and more importantly, sending in numerous attacks on German airbases, including a heavy assault on the Vannes, headquarters of KGr. 100. On 13 November, Air Intelligence reported that a German POW under interrogation had stated that an operation pending would be a three phase attack on an industrial district in the Midlands. Officers thought the prisoner meant that Umbrella was KGr. 100 and that Moonshine Serenade, the name of the actual three phase attack, and a third phase meant, 'something else.'

On 14 November at 1. p.m. Operation Coldwater, led by Air Intelligence, saw twenty-seven German air bases and beam transmitters bombed, even Berlin; and night fighters (although at this stage not effective) were on standby. This in itself makes a mockery of the conspiracy theory. On the same day an Air Intelligence secret document was prepared for Churchill telling him of Moonlight Sonata, stating, 'We believe that the target areas will be ... probably in the vicinity of London, but if further information indicates Coventry, Birmingham [based on pilot and POW story] or elsewhere, we hope to get instructions out in time.'

With hindsight we know that target 51 was Wolverhampton (not bombed), *Einheitspreis*; target 52, Birmingham (bombed 19/20 November), *Regenschirm*; and target 53, Coventry, was *Korn*. Korn had of course been mentioned once before but no one in intelligence understood its meaning. They did in fact later say that there was nothing in the decrypt to suggest that Korn concealed the identity of a target. They even suggested it referred to chaff; a foil used to confuse radar. No actual understandable source from anywhere, including Enigma, barring the captured pilot, ever stated that Coventry was an actual target. Peter Calvocoressi. Air Section Head many years later, said simply, 'Ultra never mentioned Coventry!'

R. V. Jones, the scientist in charge of counter intelligence at Bletchley, said that the signals relating to the raid were not decoded in time and that they (Bletchley) were not aware that it was the target! As he left London that night he said he was still wondering where the raid would be!

As they prepared the bombers over the Channel, this document lay on a desk, possibly in a bomb damaged airfield, dated 13 November 1940, a Secret Command Headquarters Document. These are the highlights:

Kampfgeschwader General Wever 4
Subject: Operational orders for: A) '*Mondscheinsonate*'
                                     B) '*Regenschirm*'
Enemy Situation:

See enemy Information report ... with sketch plans ... secret, dated 9.11.40. Further enemy documentation, in particular regarding defence and searchlight installation, is currently to hand.

Task:

Subject to appropriate weather conditions, it is intended to carry out two operations similar to the London ones, in which all units of *Luftflotten* 2 and 3 will participate, against:

A) Coventry
B) Birmingham

These operations will constitute large scale attacks against an important part of the English war industry. It is my expectation that during these operations the crews will maintain their previous keenly aggressive spirit.

Execution:

Actuation procedure:

For the large A operation, the attack on Coventry, the code word '*Mondscheinsonate*' (Moonlight Sonata) will be used.

For the large B operation, the attack on Birmingham, the code word '*Regenschirm*' will be used.

Timing of Attacks:
Immediate implementation is to be expected.

Strength of formations:
It is a question of committing as many planes as possible. Other assignments are to be postponed on the day of the attack.

Targets:
Care must be taken to see that there is appropriate dispersion of the formations when their attack begins, in accordance with the direction of the wind, in order that the entire target may be covered.

For attack A: [Coventry]
See moonlight chart 2.

Formation from IX *Fliegerkorps* will attack the RESPECTIVE ENTIRE TARGET [my caps].
Rath Oberleutnant

As aircrews prepared, loaded and fuelled bombers, back in England the people of Coventry were busy with another day. Sir David Hunt later informs us that his friend Sir John Colville, one of Churchill's private secretaries, was on duty at No. 10 with Churchill on that night. He said the Prime Minister set off that afternoon for Ditchley with another Private Secretary John Martin. On the way he opened the yellow Ultra Box and read the Ultra message telling him of a massive raid on an unspecified target. This is likely to be the message I mentioned before, which still suggests London but adds Coventry as a possibility. He immediately returned to London, expecting the raid there, sent his staff into the bunker and stood on the roof with General Ismay waiting for the bombers. Sir John Martin himself confirmed in 1976 that he handed Churchill the message and after reading it Churchill immediately told the driver to return to London. Sir John wrote,

> My recollection is that he explained that the German 'beam' indicated the prospect of a heavy raid on London and that he was not going to spend the night peacefully in the country when the metropolis was under heavy attack.

That was never part of Churchill's character!

The Big Raid,
14 November 1940

At 6.17 p.m. *Kampfgruppe* 100, pathfinders consisting of thirteen Heinkel 111s, droned across Lyme Bay in Dorset carrying 10,224 incendiary and forty-eight 100lb bombs which they began dropping at 7.20 p.m. precisely. According to the Chief Fire Officer of Coventry, the evening started with:

> The yellow message was received at 1905, the purple at 1908, and the Red warning at 1910. Action commenced quickly in brilliant moonlight, and the first fire was reported at 1924. Throughout the night there was no perceptible lull in the attack ... Within the first five minutes a gas main was fired in the central part of the City, providing a beacon for the early raiders. Fifty-six calls were recorded in the first half-hour, and many of the fires called for three and five pumps as First attendance, and few were single pump jobs. Previous experience of large scale raids had been that fires in the early stages were confined to one or two districts, due to what would appear to have been a straight run across the City. The tactics employed on this occasion must have differed inasmuch as in this first half-hour there were fires in six widely separated districts.

The chief felt that at 7.40 p.m. everything was under control, but by 7.59 p.m. things were getting considerably worse; all of the pumps had been called out and seventy one calls reporting fires had been received. At this time other crews from outside the city first began to arrive. By 8.02 p.m. the chief realised that the raid was unusually heavy. He wrote,

> The intensity of the bombardment increased and all reports indicated that the attack was of an unprecedented nature for a provincial town. Incendiary bombs, explosive incendiaries, oil bombs, HEs of all calibres, parachute mines and

flares were being used ... Outside aid was arriving but owing to the swiftness of developments, not quickly enough...

At 8.05 the last pathfinder passed, followed fifteen minutes later by more Heinkels dropping HEs, landmines and another 2,412 incendiaries. This was then followed every ten to fifteen minutes by batches of about twenty aircraft, Heinkels, Dornier 17s and Junkers 88s crossing the city from five directions at a height of up to 20 to 30,000 feet.

John Bailey Shelton lived in Little Park Street; he wrote,

We watched the flares dropped by the attacking planes. Rows of them seemed to hang suspended in the sky and reminded one of the fairy lights of a coronation. Suddenly a terrific hissing was heard as thousands of incendiary bombs fell ... when the flare of these firebombs died we could see the glare of burning houses ... As I returned to the stables high explosives began to fall every half minute or so and made the ground and sheds leap into the air.

Incendiary bombs exploding in the street; 30,000 fell in one night!

John soon found his home surrounded by flames!

AFS man Alec E. Clemson wrote of his memories of the night back in 1985; he then lived in Lower Mitcham, South Australia. He wrote,

As I cycled down the Daventry Road hill, flares lit up the sky and the glow growing over the city turned orange. The crew had already left and were in Broadgate, so I followed them towards the glare of the city. Leaving my cycle by the Midland Bank I went along High Street to Broadgate. There was an engine and turntable ladder up at Lloyds Bank roof. In Broadgate there were cars, trailer pumps, hoses, water jets and firemen. There was the crackle of burning wood and the shock of explosions in that ring of fire. Broadgate was aflame and I searched desperately for the crew with whom I trained, but in vain. Most of the firemen there I knew; Bill Maddocks, manager of Anslow's, was there – I think it was his car which stood outside Boots the Chemist [famously photographed blown up after the raid but restored after the war]. Owen Owen's store was ablaze and, in the glowing sparks made by falling structures in Ironmonger Row, firemen went down.

He hung onto the branch pipe which threshed him from side to side, until I reached him and grabbed it. The water pressure was strong and the branch pipe seemed alive as I mounted the entrance steps. A voice, fireman Kimberly's I believe called, 'Come on out of that -- the next floor is caving in!' I turned back to Broadgate, it was just at that moment that the next floor caved in and belched out through the doorway.

Bombs were falling and the explosions that followed their whine could be heard momentarily drowning the roar of flames and the hiss as water turned to steam. As I reached Boots there was a nearer whine of a bomb and I leaned for shelter against a car. The hit was made in Market Street, off Broadgate. The car rocked on its springs. Incendiary bombs were still bursting into flower here and there, neatly planted rows of them along the road, ignored by firemen energetically concerned with the burning buildings.

Moving nearer to the High Street Alec found another crew fighting a blaze at Astley's paint shop:

I joined a lone man doing his best to hold the branch pipe steady. The two of us managed it well enough but the heat was terrific! As I looked back towards Boots, the car by which I had stood burst into flames. There was a thin scream in the air and a red blinding blast as Astley's took another salvo. The front of the ground floor shop coughed out and the burning paint nearly made me retch. The fireman I was helping, Edgar Humphries, was knocked to his knees by the blast. He gasped, 'Can you hold it,' as I answered he staggered away to the pump ... the water pressure was failing and shortly there was no more. The mains had been hit.

Firemen doing their bit in Hertford Street. Fire fighting surrounded by fires and falling bombs resulted in fifty-seven deaths during the various bombings of Coventry.

This was later in the evening; at least an hour was then spent trying to relay pipes from the Sherbourne across shattered buildings. The river was, however, too low and no further water was forthcoming ... Broadgate had to be left to burn.

Robin Oliver of Wolverhampton some years ago gave me information on what was happening at Wolverhampton's AFS stations at this time. At 8.18 p.m. Wolverhampton AFS received a call from the Regional Commissioner for Civil Defence, saying that Coventry had been raided and to send five pumps for assistance immediately. An hour later five pumps from Wolverhampton, Coseley, Bilston and Wednesfield were on their way to Coventry. At 12.50 a.m a request was made for ten pumps to be sent to Ansty Road AFS Station in Walsgrave. These were gathered from the previous places plus Tipton and Penkridge. Apparently most of Wolverhampton's ambulances were also sent at that time, but on arriving found that most of the injured had been taken to hospital, leaving them with the job of collecting dead bodies. Bilston also sent a rescue party.

To add to his problems fires had taken hold in the roof of the fire station itself and the Control Room had to be abandoned. Water from these fires caused the

WARDEN'S REPORT FORM.   A.R.P./M.I.

Form of Report to Report Centres.

(Commence with the words)   "AIR RAID DAMAGE"

Designation of REPORTING AGENT   606.C˙
(e.g., Warden's Sector Number)

POSITION of occurrence

COAT OF ARMS BRIDGE ROAD. AT RAILWAY BRIDGE.

TYPE of bombs :—H.E.   ~~Incendiary~~   ~~Poison Gas~~

Approx. No. of CASUALTIES :— MANY, YES, BY DEBRIS.
(If any trapped under wreckage, say so)

If FIRE say so : YES, REPORTED DIRECT TO DAVENTRY ROAD.
FIRE STATION.

Damage to MAINS :— ~~Water~~ ~~Coal Gas~~ ~~Overhead electric cables~~ ~~Sewers~~

Names of ROADS BLOCKED

COAT O F ARMS BRIDGE ROAD.   DEBRIS.

Position of any UNEXPLODED BOMBS

NONE.

Time of occurrence (approx.)   20.25 HOURS.

Services already ON THE SPOT or COMING :—

N.F.S.

Remarks :— DIRECT HIT ON PASSENGER TRAIN.

BRIDGE DEMOLISHED.

APPROACH VIA KENILWORTH ROAD.

(Finish with the words)   "MESSAGE ENDS"

ORIGINAL   These words are for use with a report sent by messenger.
DUPLICATE   Delete whichever does not apply.

This ARP report went in at 8.25 p.m. on the night of 14 November. There was a direct hit on a passenger train and the bridge was demolished in Coat of Arms Bridge Road. The National Fire Service were attending or going to attend.

switchboard itself to become live and at 8.00 p.m. all the telephone lines failed, the main lighting failed and the emergency lighting itself was badly affected. Two lines survived but were unreliable.

An unnamed Burnley man, in Coventry on war work, told the press:

When the first German raiders appeared over the city I was just starting an eight-mile cycle ride to work. Needless to say, this was a hair-raising ride. Although I was in France during the last war I've never experienced anything like the Coventry raid. The Alert sounded as me and a workmate began our journey, but we decided to continue anyway. We had been riding about five minutes when the first incendiaries dropped; it was a real firework display, with flashes, cracks, and bangs all over the place. Several times we had throw ourselves down at the side of the road when an aircraft appeared overhead and bombs were heard whistling through the air, some falling in fields not far distant. Several times I have cycled through raids, but never have I experienced a ride like this one. The planes came over wave after wave, and there was not a quiet minute. When bombs were not failing you could still hear the drone of the planes.

Harry James recalls being present when the raid started:

Mr Hicks, our local air raid warden, lived opposite our house in Junction Street; he knocked on the door to tell my mother it was going to be a bad night as there was a full moon. Dad had told us to sit in the cubby hole under the stairs until he got back. Mum told Mr Hicks that she would wait for Dad to get home then head for the air raid shelter beneath the Old Rudge Works in Spon Street. Eventually Dad arrived and although he was not keen to go to the shelter Mum persuaded him!

As we passed the Old Globe pub an incendiary bomb just missed Mum's head and hit a pile of sand nearby! Finally, with Dad carrying me in his arms, we entered the shelter; he wanted to leave us there and go back home [many men chose to return home to protect it] but by now the raid was getting worse and he took us deeper into the shelter! It was one of the main shelters and was full of men, women and children. In the deep areas were iron escape hatches which were closed as there were fears of flooding from the River Sherbourne close by! Many of my school friends were also there and, being so young, didn't realise the danger! Suddenly I was gripped from behind and lifted into the air to look into someone's blackened face, whose eyes were bright red, cheeks streaked with tears. Terrified I eventually recognised Mr Hicks the warden!

We soon found Mum and Dad to be told our home was no more, just a pile of rubble. It appeared that he and others had been digging in the debris looking for Mum and me!!! And as the bombing became worse had to give up. Mr Hicks thought he would never see us alive again!

At seven o'clock the Provost of Coventry, the Very Revd R. T. Howard, met his firewatchers on the roof of the nave of St Michael. They consisted of the cathedral's stone mason, Jock Forbes, who usually stayed with the Provost all night, and Mr Wright and W. H. Eaton. The Provost recalled that within as little as five minutes after the siren sounded the bombers could be heard approaching, and soon a half circle of light appeared over the city as the many fires took hold. At 7.40 a.m. the first incendiary hit the cathedral, one fell on the roof of the chancel and another pierced the roof and fell into the nave by the lectern. Another took hold on the roof of the south aisle above the organ. One of the men shouted across the road to the nearby police station to call for a fire crew. The bomb above the chancel was flipped over the battlements and the one in the nave covered in two buckets of sand and shovelled up. The incendiary, however, over the south aisle had burned through the lead and fallen into the inner roof and was starting to burn the timber. This took all four men to deal with it, lead was hacked up and sand poured in, but the fire had spread beyond the sand so stirrup pumps were brought into action, more lead was ripped up and bucket after bucket of water was pumped in before it was brought under control.

Another stick of incendiaries followed; one burst through the roof of the Capper's chapel and started a furious blaze. This was subdued with difficulty as water and

Bailey Lane burning, taken on the morning of 15 November.

sand was running short and took time to move from one place to another; more refills were needed and the four fire fighters had a large and complex area to cover. While the men were fighting fires on the roof, parts of the clerestory windows were blasted over them from the force of a nearby HE hitting.

Meanwhile another bomb had fallen on the north aisle above the Smith's chapel, the light of which could be seen from the south side through the clerestory windows. Only one of the crew could be spared to deal with it and luckily it was easily dealt with. The bombs dealt with, the men took a breather, then another shower of incendiaries fell; four hit the roof of the Girdler's chapel above the north aisle and took hold in the ceiling, leaving holes punched through the lead with smoke pouring out. Of this, afterwards the Provost said:

> These again were tackled by all four of us at once, but with the failing of our supplies of sand and water, and physical strength, we were unable to make an impression, the fire gained strength, and ultimately we had to give in. During all this period of nearly an hour when we were extinguishing bombs we were hoping every minute for the arrival of the fire brigade, yet we could hardly be surprised that none came, for the whole of Coventry seemed ablaze.

Smoke was issuing out of the spiral staircase back down into the cathedral, forcing the men to get down via a long ladder placed on the north side after the hit on 14 October. One of the men tried to get more water from the only source, a tap by the north aisle, and was nearly overcome with smoke and had to be helped back. The Provost continued, 'Looking inside the north door, the roof above the Children's chapel could be seen well ablaze.' The men set about saving what they could; they rescued the pewter cross and candlesticks from the Smith's chapel. Next they went into the sanctuary and vestries to rescue more items, taking the cross and candlesticks from the high altar, paten, chalice etc., which they took to the nearby police station. Then the Provost said,

> we all four went together to the south porch to rest and wait under cover for the fire brigade, wrapping ourselves in blankets ... for we were streaming with perspiration, though the night was cold. We found it really more frightening to be waiting there inactive with high explosives falling near than to be active in the open.

At 9.30 the Solihull Fire Brigade arrived and laid pipes everywhere, helped by an unknown sixteen-year-old boy, who, bare headed, seemed more than willing despite the danger. A hose was hauled up a ladder and played over the north porch; liquid lead was running off the roof! Then suddenly the water stopped; the fire crew linked onto another hydrant in Priory Street but nothing, the mains had gone and that was it ... nothing could be done to save the great building. The Provost recalled,

Coventry's much loved cathedral still burning the following morning. Note the crossed timbers are these the ones which Jock Forbes wired together?

A final look through the north door showed a new fire blazing high up in the roof of the nave, where evidently another incendiary bomb had been burning for some time out of sight. And a wide area of the pews was burning. At this time, unknown to the Provost, a policeman and soldier had climbed up onto the roof and were throwing incendiaries off the battlements. The police officer had to leave injured, after an exploding incendiary had blasted phosphorous into his face! The Provost looked through the doors for the last time and saw the beautiful medieval pews on fire; they were due to be removed in three days time! At 10.30 a.m. the water came back on and the fire crew managed to play water upon the Lady Chapel, the pressure however was low and again it gave out. At this time there was a loud crash, maybe the roof falling or an HE, and the fire crew retired; the Provost grabbed the colours of the Royal Warwickshire Regiment from the blazing building.

My own father, Cyril McGrory, then in a reserved occupation, was in the Radford Hotel when the raid started. All the people in the pub eventually made their way into the cellar. Not one to take shelter during raids my Dad left the pub and stood outside watching the fireworks. He said there were massive explosions everywhere and shrapnel raining out of the sky, when suddenly he saw high up a parachute drifting down. Thinking that a Jerry had bailed out, he was just thinking of going after it when he realised there was a large container attached to it … it was a land mine! The mine was above St Nicholas' church opposite. Dad was still taking in the scene; it blew, downwards and out, leaving just one course of stones standing at the base of the church. Dad was blown off his feet and when he could get his bearings he headed straight over to the church knowing that people, scouts and fire guards were sheltering in its crypt. Dad began to pull away at the rubble and eventually was able to drag the injured out. Now he needed to move them so he looked over towards the road and saw a car, open topped with big runner boards, as it came weaving its way up the Radford Road around the debris. He jumped down and told the driver what was going on then started to get the injured into the car. He then stood on the runner as the driver, avoiding the bombs and craters, took them through to St George's Church Relief Station on Coundon Road. They then went back and repeated the journey many times as the bombs fell until all the injured survivors were safe … what Dad did afterwards he never said, but no doubt made sure Gran and Grandad and the rest of the family were safe in the shelters. Then he eventually got home, only to find a large lump of concrete had gone through his bed! This wouldn't be the only

My dad, Cyril McGrory; he did his bit during the bombing of Coventry and on foreign shores. Commandos were executed if captured!

time Dad was blown up for during another raid he was blown 40 feet across the road outside the shops in Cramper's Fields, Radford. This time when he dusted himself off, he walked passed a pair of woman's legs still standing in a shop doorway! The following morning the dead were laid out on the grass, covered in tarpaulin. Dad had had enough, he joined the Marines and became a commando and fought with Combined Ops and Special Services in many places including Norway, Sword Beach and Salerno in Italy, where he was strafed in the legs by a Stuka dive bomber!

The Revd Clitheroe knew nothing of my Dad's involvement with his 'daughter' church, he wrote,

> Our daughter church of St Nicholas, Radford was completely obliterated by a heavy bomb, and the curate in charge of the fire guard (the Revd John Lister) had been blinded. The young men constructed the guard were killed. I know of no incident of this tragic night worse than this. But these young men died hero's deaths in the discharge of their sacred duty.

Two days later the King himself would be standing at these ruins and visiting St George's!

Brenda Mendenhall recalled that at the time,

> On 14 November I went with my father to the Astoria Cinema in Albany Road. The raid started after seven but we stayed till the end of the film, *Hurricane*. When we came out we ran to a brick shelter in Kensington Road, stayed an hour, then ran to another in Bristol Road. Then on to the underground one on Hearsall Common, where we spent the rest of the night until 7.00 a.m. when we walked home to Sherlock Road. The only damage was a broken kitchen window! I discovered afterwards that each street shelter we left was bombed afterwards!

Another cinema goer was Bill Tisdale on his night off from his FAP, First Aid Post, in Coundon. Bill told me in 2010,

> That night I had decided on a visit to the Gaumont. Around 7.15 p.m. I heard the sirens; this had happened so many times without result that I became a little blasé, and just carried on watching the film. After about half an hour it sounded like all hell had been let loose outside, I found out later that an anti aircraft unit was operating in Whitefriars Street, and every time the gun went off the vibration shook plaster onto the stage. After about twenty minutes the manager, Mr Hugh Denton, came onto the stage and told the audience that a heavy raid was in progress and would everybody move to the back of the cinema. I decided to go a little further and entered the foyer; I sat myself on the floor facing towards the cinema and a little to the right of the doors. I am sure this action resulted in saving

my life for sometime later, the doors suddenly blew open and a cloud of red dust poured through. There was an Air Force person standing right outside these doors and he spun around like a top, afterwards dropping to the floor. Upon examining him I found him to be dead, incidentally the red dust turned out to be the red plush off the seats, the blast from the bomb had obviously caused this.

Bill continued,

Mr Denton appeared on the scene and I asked him if he had any bandages or dressings, then he and I ventured into the cinema to look for survivors, there was a gaping hole in the roof over the stage and a huge hole just in front of it, inside I found two more dead people. The manager then suggested that the remaining people went under the front foyer, and throughout the night people were entering, sobbing and deploring the loss of their homes. I had no choice but to endure a total of eleven hours bombing. I couldn't get out, everything being on fire and wardens were preventing anyone leaving because of the presence of delayed action bombs.

Stan Morris recalled this night in their Anderson shelter,

My father went to open the door just to have a quick look. As he did so there was an enormous explosion that threw him back over us. It must have been the land mine that landed on the shops at the corner of Cramper's Field which demolished them. At about 1.30 a.m. all went quiet again for about 15 minutes and suddenly there was a banging and shouting outside, someone was shouting, 'Let us in.' It was Peter Annis and his mother and father from 121 Moseley Avenue. They had been sheltering under the table. We let them in and then there were seven of us crammed into the small shelter.

Martyn Hammond recalled to me a few years ago his memories of the night. He begins:

The 14 November blitz was an experience of its own. It started early and we didn't have time to put our bits and pieces in the street shelter to make it comfortable. Our evening meal was left on the table and our pet dog, Jock, was left tied up under the kitchen sink. One thing that remains with me is the sight of three parachute flares descending like huge chandeliers above us. Shortly after came the bombs. Behind our house was the railway line, then Smith's Stampings works and then the Humber works. I still remember the scream of the bomb that exploded in the middle of St George's Road only a few yards away. It left a huge crater and destroyed six houses. If the bomb blast had come our way it would have demolished our shelter. We all laid flat on the ground in our shelter and the blast went through, above our heads and took the two blankets away we had hung over

Bomb damaged houses on the Radford Road.

the doors! Our house was also hit and we were worried about our dog, Jock, who had broken loose and was running around in the house, barking. Mother wouldn't let us out of the shelter to fetch him because of the intensity of the bombing. Air raid Wardens kept popping in to see us and told us the centre of the city and cathedral had been destroyed.

At 10.30 a.m. PC Wilfred Lambert returned to the police station in St Mary's Street. He later recalled,

All this time bombs were falling, and when I went into the station the doors were flying backwards and forwards by the terrific blast that was going through the building, like a whirlwind. Most of the windows had been blown out and the blinds were flapping. Nearly all our telephones had been put out of action, so that the few reports that came through were delivered by hand. A message came to say that a shelter under Smith's the Furnishers in Jordan Well had been hit and fourteen people were trapped underneath. A volunteer rescue party was formed, and PC Rollins, Timms, four specials, inspector Ward and myself went. I worked relief, and most of the digging was done by the PCs. If ever two men deserved a medal they did, but they did not even know their efforts were all in vain. They both took off their coats and were working in shirt sleeves, tunnelling under huge piles of debris with spades

Streets in central Coventry still smoking.

and pickaxes. After about an hour, I was asked by PC Rollins to try to get some more help from the Police Station. I had just reached there when Inspector Ward staggered along St. Mary's Street and said that the rescue party had all been killed by a direct hit. I went with him and saw all five of the rescue party lying on top of a heap of bricks and debris. They were all blackened and burned, but recognisable ... This proved that a bomb can fall in the same place twice, contrary to all sayings.

PC Lambert continued,

The heat from the surrounding fires at this time was terrific ... brick ends and rubble were flying through the air, and it was so light you could see buildings collapsing, right and left. The streets of the town were deserted by this time and as I made my way up Gosford Street, from the GEC fire it seemed like hell on earth. I slowly made my way over heaps of debris and round bomb craters to the Police Station. It seemed almost laughable to be putting out incendiaries while the whole city burned. When I arrived at the station I could see the roof of the cathedral had collapsed, and showers of sparks and flames were coming out of it. The police station was surrounded by fire, every building along Jordan Well, Earl Street, Hay

Lane and Bayley Lane was ablaze. It was impossible to try to put out all the fires... standing in St Mary's street I saw several land mines floating down by parachute. They could be easily seen in the light of the fires, and one or two actually exploded in mid-air, probably by the bullets which were being fired at them.

At 11.30 a.m., back at the cathedral, the whole building was ablaze sending massive copper coloured flames souring into the sky; the bells continued chiming the hours. At this time the Provost was sheltering in the porch of the police station with a dozen men of the Solihull Auxiliary Fire Service. Here they watched the cathedral burn, while high explosives were falling everywhere. The great steel strengthening bands placed in the cross beams were twisting in the heat and pulling the great columns down, collapsing into the church and tearing the remaining roof down with it. The Provost recalled, 'The whole interior was a seething mass of flame and piled up blazing beams and timbers, interpenetrated and surmounted with dense bronzed coloured smoke. Through this could be seen the organ, famous for its long history back to the time when Handel played upon it.'

Over thirty thousand feet above this scene at precisely the same time above the roaring red glow that was Coventry, encompassed in a rolling, stuttering drone, was Willy Monk, a wireless operator in a Heinkel 111. Willy wrote of his experience,

This evening it's the big raid, Moonlight Sonata, a major raid on a centre of the British war industry, namely Coventry. We are among those who took off last [the planes came from a number of bases]. Weather very good, clear sky with good moon. We will soon be over the channel. We are flying in a single line, one after the other, following Anton (beam signal). The sky is so clear we hardly need Anton --- almost like daylight. We are past the main signal and our bombers are ready for dropping. We are carrying high explosives bombs and incendiaries. We count off the distance until we are over the city. It is 23.30 – the city is already burning. I feel for the neck chain that my mother gave me. We hardly notice when our bombs are dropped automatically. Although we are flying at 10,000 meters we can smell the city burning below. We can see the red glow in the sky almost all the way back to Bourges.

Monk made it safely back but one bomber didn't; a Dornier 17 belonging to *Luftflotte* II (No. DO 17Z3, 5K+BP) was shot down by ack ack fire at Loughborough and crashed at Prestwold Hall, Burton on the Wolds, at 10 o'clock. The crew of four were all killed and were buried at Loughborough. A Birmingham ack-ack crew also claimed to have shot a German plane down that night but no wreckage was ever found to confirm it.

Monk's bomber had passed over the city and more replaced it. In one of the crypts of the cathedral, sheltering, were woman and children; the Provost mentions their removal at 12.30 but nothing else; however a letter in the MDT states,

A downed Dornier 17 from a Coventry address! Is this the Dornier shot down on 14 November?

There was one point in the burning of the cathedral which the Provost missed, and that was the pluck and coolness of those women and children who were in the crypt. Never did I see any troops cooler during my two and a half years on the Western Front than those woman and children. While the fire was raging above them they were singing. When the roof fell (there were two falls which sounded like the roll of thunder) the children jumped up, which was only natural as they did not know about the fire that was burning above them, but there was no panic and they sat down again. When the time came for the people to be moved I thought what a terrible test it was going to be for those women and children. Out they came in their family groups, no panic, no crying, just the same spirit as they showed in the crypt. Yours faithfully,
E. W. Ansell.

The city was being slowly torn apart. Bomber pilot Cajus Bekker looked down on the burning mass from his bomber and later wrote, 'The usual cheers that greeted a direct hit stuck in our throats. The crew just gazed down on the sea of flames in silence. Was this really a military target?'

Back in Broadgate, our AFS man, Alec, had struggled on amid the fire and bombs. 'At least an hour was spent trying to relay pipes from the Sherbourne across shattered buildings; the river was, however, too low and no further water was forthcoming ... Broadgate had to be left to burn.' Alec recalled,

Someone said that hundreds of people had been drowned in the Co-op shelters when the mains burst. Others told us that the cathedral had been destroyed. We cursed the bastards overhead! Broadgate was still a ring of fire, while above the drone of planes still registered in our awareness. My face was red and sore from the heat and was to remain so for days. The whole shopping area was aflame, Boots and Samuel's were both down ... Lyon's upper storey had fallen. Owen Owen's ruins went skywards as another stick of bombs hit them dead centre. The fire crews had left Broadgate and only several unattached men like myself were left trying to stem the lesser fires... It was 1.00 a.m. and there was seemed little one could do, so I decided to see how my family had fared.

At the Coventry and Warwickshire Hospital, the House Governor reported,

Two big fires were started. The emergency dressing store which adjoins the ward block was hit by incendiaries and the fire spread rapidly. Almost immediately the

Probably the only surviving photograph of Coventry burning on the night of 14 November. The glow over the city could be seen by the bombers crossing the Channel.

main dressing store was also hit and was soon blazing fiercely. Onwards throughout the night, bombing was incessant. We fought fire in various wards. Patients were moved from one building to another always just in time, and miraculously there were no casualties among the hospital patients or staff. Soon after midnight, the electric current failed. Operations were continued in three theatres with the emergency lighting. The windows of two theatres were blown in. It was soon too cold to continue operating in these, but work was carried on in the one remaining theatre.

As the night wore on it became bitterly cold in all the wards, as every window had long since been blown out. Extra blankets were issued. Every few moments we had to throw ourselves on the floor as tremendous explosions shook the buildings, we thought that every brief lull must mark the end of the raid, but by about three o'clock we seemed to realise that only the coming dawn – still several hours away – would end it. The one operating theatre in use could not cope with the large number of cases transferred from the reception hall, and casualties covered almost every foot of floor space in the lower rooms and corridors. Nursing staff moved about the clinic by the light of hurricane lamps comforting the injured and giving small drinks of water. The staff and patients were magnificent. There was never a sign of panic, and several of the male patients were continuously in the grounds putting out incendiary bombs. In one ward, badly shattered by a high explosive bomb less than 20 yards away, patients who could not moved were lying in their beds watching the planes in the sky, which was aglow from the fires in the city.

It was reported by Dr Herry Winter in *Life* magazine that on that night,

Throughout the packed hospital, there was not one cry of fear, not one sign of panic. We did not have a case of hysteria all night long. The only word of complaint came from a wounded German airman who had been in the hospital for few days. He was on the top floor of the main building. When the orderlies finally went to him they found him cringing in bed and muttering in English, 'Too much bomb – too long – too much bomb.'

Among those in the hospital was worker, forty-five-year-old Joseph Leonard Holms of Barnoldswick. He was also a volunteer ARP man and was on sentry duty at a shelter when the steel door was blown into him by a high explosive bomb. Leonard would survive the night, but died on Sunday.

Valerie East's father worked on nights at the Daimler, Radford, making Lancaster bomber parts; he travelled from Northampton everyday by train to his night shift. When the train pulled into the station on the night of 14 November he and others were rounded up by police and bussed to the hospital to help, 'with the bodies and patients'. At 1.00 a.m. antiquarian and archaeologist John Bailey Shelton was watching his house and library collapse in on itself in Little Park Street, in it were about 500 books including many rare Coventry volumes and old deeds, maps and engravings of old Coventry. Luckily his museum survived!

At about 1.20 a.m. our AFS man Alec arrived home. He recalled,

As I reached the house I was nearly faint with apprehension. The roof was gaping, windows were broken, a door was down, the house next door was badly damaged. I could not describe my feelings when I found them both safe under the stairs, scared but outwardly calm. 'Daddy, the bombs fell right by us!' Excitedly cried my little daughter. Marjorie told me that Helen had slept some of the time but I don't suppose her eyes closed at all. As I stood, hesitating, my wife said, 'Still on duty?' I nodded, 'I must get back to the Broadgate shelters.' She cut some sandwiches in the dark and settled under the stairs again ... I kissed them and returned to Broadgate ... Several wardens collected gear as flames licked out of the upper windows of the King's Head Hotel... I ran through the foyer, up flights of stairs to the top landing followed by a warden. We turned on taps in the bathrooms but they were dry... We opened every bedroom door to check for occupants... Two maids, fully dressed, and a waiter emerged, scared to death... we found no one else. The landing was filled with acrid smoke as we ran downstairs. 'Just a minute,' I called, 'Let's take Tom out – he ought to have a chance.' The warden came back up a few steps up the first floor lounge, where in a glass case, stood the life sized wooden figure of Peeping Tom... Axes are handy, we soon had Tom down the stairs. 'I'll take him to Cheylesmore as a mascot,' I joked, but Tom was heavier than I thought and would not bend! It took both of us to carry him across Hertford Street. We leaned Tom on a post outside Walker's the Jewellers [corner of the Nat West], where he was found at daylight, unharmed and still unbending. The national papers had his photograph the next day.

He then ran to the yard of the King's Head to the shelters where, 'we told the warden to take his 'flock' to the shelters at Greyfriar's Green, where there was less danger of fire. Alec continues,

against the glow in Broadgate, the figure of a fireman showed, stumbling I made towards him. It was Bill Tromans from Cheylesmore, looking for his crew from whom he had been cut off. He had been hit by something and the next thing he knew was he was on the other side of town. Noel's and Whitfields were nearly burned down and looking across the tram lines at them, I remembered that air-raid shelters were under Noel's. We hurried towards them; the heat was almost too much for us, but we found the shelter opening. I called down, 'Come on out you'll roast alive, there's a shelter under the Midland Bank.' No one budged, but at last after some persuasion two nurses emerged. They would not come with us; instead they scurried off to the Coventry and Warwickshire Hospital, their capes over their

Peeping Tom; not the photo from the press but another. Tom looking rather annoyed on the morning of 15 November.

heads. Others in the shelter did at last come out, obviously deeply scared. Bill and I escorted them to the Midland Bank in Little Park Street. There was little activity in the sky as we made the two journeys.

At this point Bill Troman had had enough and rested in the shelter and Alec decided to return to his AFS Fire Station in Cheylesmore. He carried his bike over the rubble in Little Park Street and as he passed Bushell's bricks rained down on him bouncing off his bike and helmet, stunning him slightly. He arrived at the Cheylesmore station at 3.00 a.m. and found the Whitley crew there, exhausted, sleeping using their respirators as pillows. Alec settled down with them.

At 1.30 a.m. John Shelton was coaxing his terrified horses out of their stable away from approaching fire,

Crash after crash followed every few moments and now most of the roofs were fallen in. The falling walls, girders, pillars, machinery [in the next door Swift factory] crashing four storeys, the droning of the planes as they let go of their bombs, and the rattling of the shrapnel on the corrugated sheeting was deafening all night long. It beggars description. The drifting fires were worse, and one had to guess where the noise like thunder came from. I found out afterwards that it had been the crashing of the pillars of the cathedral. It was hell let loose; no one could possibly have lived in our street.

Philip Deeming lived by the GEC Telephone Works in Stoke and recalled,

A bomb hit a block of four houses a few yards from our house killing all the residents, including those in their garden shelters. Doors were blown off, and all the windows were smashed in the neighbouring houses. We had a brick built surface shelter in the garden and I can still 'see' my mother going into the shelter every time the sirens sounded, taking her knitting bag with her insurance policies, documents, etc. and the budgerigar in his cage. During the height of the bombing, nerves were beginning to fray and at one period she was holding the wall of the shelter with her hands forlornly, hoping to prevent it from being blown on top of us. Fortunately we survived – perhaps it worked!

The last bombs, about a dozen 100-pounders, were dropped at 5.30 a.m. in Shortley Road off the London Road. The Rattigan family were in their Anderson; Maurice Rattigan recalls the event,

Near dawn a dozen or so nearby explosions shook our shelter and we could hear debris falling all around. Ignoring the danger we left the shelter and in the moonlight could see rubble all around us. The side entry was full of debris and we

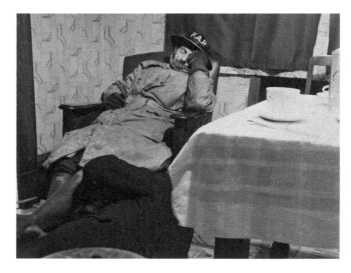

An exhausted First Aid Post man grabbing sleep while he can. The photograph taken by James Armer would place him in the Stoney Stanton Road area.

clambered over it to the front of the house where we saw absolute carnage. The majority of bombs had fallen in the road outside our house, but one had taken the bay window of No. 9 and at No. 13 opposite the complete front was missing. Two doors away from us at No. 4 where the Knibbs family lived, the front of the house was also missing. A house down the street also had the back of the property blown away and a street shelter had a direct hit, but fortunately it was empty. But not so fortunate were the occupants of the street shelter outside No. 2, which was demolished and the eight occupants were all injured. As we surveyed the carnage three figures emerged from the damaged house opposite. The young couple had the wife's elderly father staying and he stumbled across the rubble with a saucepan on his head ... he looked a pathetic figure being led through the rubble and we took him to our shelter. There were no more bombs that night; as we emerged from the shelter we heard the engines of the departing plane that had turned our quiet little street into a battlefield. We later found our mantel piece clock had stopped at 5.30 a.m.

The all-clear finally came at 6.15 a.m. The result of this raid was 568 dead, 863 severely injured and 343 slightly injured. Of houses, 2,294 were destroyed, 5,602 uninhabitable and 29,374 damaged. Schools, cinemas, pubs and shops were also destroyed and thirty-five small and large factories targeted. There were 300 breaks in the gas mains and 200 in the water mains, and from today Coventry's tram system ceased! Coventry and its people had suffered one of the most intensive bombings in history!

Aftermath

On 15 November, as people wandered the smashed, smoke filled remains of the city, German radio was bragging about the raid.

> The raids by 500 German bombers on Coventry at one stroke destroyed the skyscraper of illusions built up by Churchill. German thoroughness used to be a byword abroad. It is true we do not like half measures, particularly when we are taking revenge. For British blockade, German blockade – for Munich, Coventry!

The following day it was announced again, more specifically referring to the raid as 'a violent blow in return for the abortive British raid on the Party celebration in Munich'. On 18 November the Germans again claimed that 500 raiders took part. The *Deutsche Allgemeine Zeitung* said with the usual German rhetoric, 'Coventry was the first to be eradicated, and that there would be a systematic and relentless decimation.' The city, they said, had been Coventrated! The number of bombers which came over the city is debatable, and at the time was said to be anything from 330 to of course 500! As the records of *Luftflotte* 2 from that night are lost, the true figure will never be known!

Eric Bramwell, who had been on fire watch in the Council House, wrote one of my favourite quotes on this morning,

> Fires still burning, unchecked; all around the city centre, craters and rubble in the streets. The devastation is indescribable. Service personal make their way slowly over the debris. No one speaks. My personal feeling is one of sadness. Then I recall the starling trilling a few notes of song as Entwhistle and I left the Council House this morning. Did the heat of the fires make the bird think it was spring, or could this be a message of hope for the future.

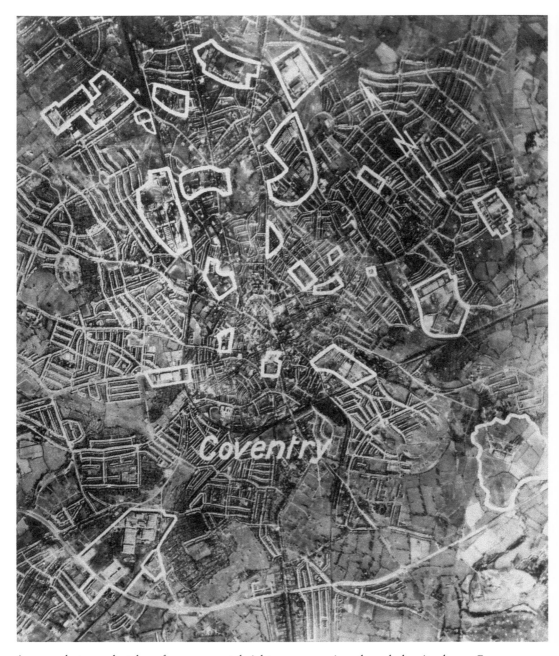

A rare photograph taken from a great height encompassing the whole city by a German reconnaissance plane as soon as the smoke cleared. The factories have been highlighted. The devastation below shows as a slight blur at this height.

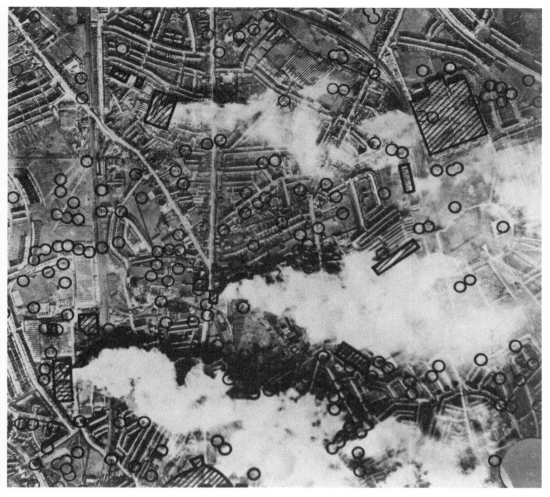

A recon shot of the Foleshill area with factories still burning. Note every bomb strike that they can see has been circled. The burning factory, top left, is between Lockhurst Lane and Foleshill Road.

Of that morning, PC Wilfred Lambert, who had been on duty since before the raid started, said,

At 6.15 a.m. the 'White' was received, but the sirens were unable to sound the 'All Clear', owing to there being no power. At about 7 a.m. a few workers and spectators began to walk the streets, and what a sight it must have been for those who had spent the whole of the eleven hour raid down the shelters. It was indescribable. Fire engines and ambulances were coming from the neighbouring towns, some had been coming in during the raid, and several fire-crews were wiped out even before they finished travelling. When daylight came, a huge black pall of smoke hung over the city, the buildings were still collapsing, right and left. I then met a rescue and ambulance party from Birmingham, in Smithford Street. I had to take them through fires and over debris until we reached Grosvenor Road, where we set about rescuing some people under a house which had received a direct hit from an HE. We only fetched out one alive, the other three lay twisted and all covered with dust and plaster, trapped by the ground floor, which had fallen in on them as they sheltered in the cellar. I then walked back to the police station; as I came up Hertford Street the heat from the fires was terrific. There were a few sightseers about but this time, but all roads to the city had been closed and only essential services allowed. It was a pitiful sight at the police station when I arrived; people were gathering and asking for information. Some had lost their homes, others had lost their relations, everybody looked tired and weary, but no one appeared to be worrying about sleep. I then went to Priory Street where there was an unexploded bomb in the road and remained there till 2.30 p.m.

Harry James recalls,

Finally after many hours the all clear was given and we were allowed out into Spon Street or what was left of it. The road was criss-crossed with hosepipes and rubble, many hoses spouted fountains of water, damaged by jagged splinters of shrapnel; many collected by us youngsters as trophies, which also included the fins of incendiary bombs. Firemen and Policemen and ambulance people stood about in tired groups and I recall blankets covering people lying on the floor. Mum said they were asleep! My eyes stung with the smoke and soon we stood in front of what was our home! It was still smoking, and then I remembered my pet cat, Tom. He was last seen in our kitchen curled up by the fireplace! A lady from nearby took us to her house and gave us tea, bread and jam. Finally a family friend took us in for a week or two and we were given clothes.

James Taylor of the *Coventry Standard* wrote,

What remains of Broadgate on the morning of 15 November.

I made my way along Barker Butts Lane, among debris of all kinds. The main water pipe from Coundon Reservoir had been fractured and stood up like a factory chimney. The houses opposite had been seriously damaged and I had to walk through a foot of water. I was accompanied by my Labrador, who like other animals had a most frightening night. Passing Bablake School I could see that much damage had been done there and that an underground shelter had a direct hit. All the way to the Council House I saw damage of all kinds, shops, whose windows had been blown out, openly displaying their wares. In front of the Council House all the property was ablaze, and it looked like the Council House, which had suffered serious damage, was doomed. The staff were busy removing important documents and papers to the basement and when I called on the town clerk (the late Mr Frederick Smith), who was an ardent Coventrian, I found him in tears.

Frederick Smith, a keen Coventry historian, wrote a fine book, *Six Hundred Years of Municipal Life,* in 1945.

Bill Tisdale spent the night trapped in the bombed Gaumont Cinema. He recalled,

An amazing view taken near the Council house, probably of Much Park Street as the dome of the Gaumont can be seen behind.

The all clear sounded, what a blessed relief, I will never forget the sight that confronted me on stepping outside, where virtually everything around the cinema was flattened or burning. It was a nightmare picking my way across the rubble. I tried walking between the Library and Trinity Church but the flames from the library were licking the walls of the church, this being a good 30 feet, so I walked past on the other side of the church; a tree was lying across Priory Row, which I had to climb over. Then the sight that greeted my eyes was the centre of the city in absolute ruin. Tears ran down my face, this was the city I had loved and where I was born! I had to, of course, walk home since there was no transport. I lived at 47 Bulwer Road at the time, and while walking up Heathcote Street my heart was in my mouth, hoping that my home was OK. It was, albeit a few slates off the roof and broken windows from a landmine that exploded nearby. Our whole family that night were separated; me in the cinema, my dad in the shelter in the garden, my Mum in the Whitmore Hotel, Sadler Road and my sister at a friend's in Fillongley. I have only visited the cinema once since, and to be quite honest I can't believe I got through it all unscathed, the memories of that awful night will stay with me forever.

That morning, my Dad wandered around the ruined city centre and returned home with a live incendiary bomb which he found wedged between two half collapsed walls. We looked for it when my Gran died in the last place it was seen, the coal house!

Our AFS man Alec Clemson's final memory concludes:

At 6.30 a.m. a call came from the Humber Works... The Control Room under the front lawn had been hit, the room had been exposed and the Control Officer was still sat at his desk! A slab of concrete had crushed the table down onto his legs, pinning him down. Out came the ropes ... we had him free in no time; that control officer was later awarded an honour in the King's List. We returned to Cheylesmore, part-time fire fighters were told to go home and sleep, there's always tonight and they'll be damping down later today. It was about 7.30 a.m., I cycled to Morningside. Marjorie and Helen were more than thankful to see me, and how good it was to see them both safe and sound. I was proud of them both, they had waited all night, alone... I ate breakfast, drank tea made with rainwater from the soft water butt and heated over a coal fire... Removing my boots and belt, I slept on a real bed, the first time for weeks. Voices awakened me at 11.00 a.m.; my mother-in-law and her sister had come to see if we were still alive. They found it very difficult getting through town, having come four miles from Keresley, walking and stumbling for over three hours, a valiant effort... As I rolled off the bed I heard my mother-in-law say, 'Duty! Did you say duty? I've never heard such a thing, his duty is with his family.' My mother-in-law was always one for the family, bless her. But I think my wife understood, later, if not then, that a man has to do what he feels he must. Discretion being the better part of honour, I slipped quietly away for damping down.

Vera Butler worked at the Post Office in Hertford Street and spent the night in the vaults below. When the all clear was given, staff were allowed to leave. Her daughter Veronica Ward recalled to me,

My mother set off to walk home to St Christians Road in Cheylesmore. As she walked down Greyfriar's Lane she was shocked to see the scenes of devastation. A bridge that had linked the Holbrooks Furniture Store was on fire and she had to run underneath to avoid the burning debris. It was a difficult walk home but fortunately the house was still standing. My mother was anxious to contact her grandmother, who lived in Stephen Road off Abbotts Lane. After another

Looking up Broadgate on the morning of 15 November. The photograph is taken from the top of the flower bed in front of Holy Trinity Church.

Fireman still trying to control fires, finding water where they could on the morning of 15 November.

difficult walk across the devastation she arrived at her mother's house which had been totally destroyed, and looters were taking items out of the debris. My Grandma was nowhere to be found. She eventually established that grandma was sheltering in St Mark's Vicarage in King William Street. Upon arrival she knocked on the door and asked the vicar about her mother. To her shock and amazement the vicar was very annoyed and referred to all the disruption of the vicarage caused by all the people taking shelter there! My mother in no uncertain terms told the vicar to stop complaining and think himself lucky to be alive and to have a home to go to! Happily my mother was reunited with my grandmother.

John Bailey Shelton wrote,

After twelve hours of this terror, hungry, tired and sleepy people emerged from their shelters as daylight began to show. Birds that had survived (not many I fear) came forth as usual for their breakfast. Cats and dogs stood outside their homes, mystified and finding them gone. My cat, which must have been in the house and probably escaped when I opened the kitchen door, had its tail scorched. It was not until several weeks later that we found him being fed by some workmen on a bombed site.

Interestingly, weeks later an RSPCA officer pointed out that there were no crazed dogs wandering the ruins of Coventry and on the night of 14 November the cat population had left the city wholesale and took several weeks to round up!

Gill Stew, who lived in Holbrooks, said,

On the night of the big blitz we were asked by a family called Worthington to share their shelter, but mother decided we would take our chance and stay at home. Thank God we did as they took a direct hit and were killed. In the morning my mother took me on my three wheeled bike all along the Foleshill Road to see what damage had occurred. As we got to Eagle Street the smell of burning wood and the clouds of dust were dreadful. We were told by locals that the cathedral had taken the full force and for us to not go any nearer.

Philip Deeming, who lived by the GEC, recalled, 'That raid left us with no water or gas, but the GEC brought us Bowsers and allowed the local residents to fetch fresh water from them until the mains were repaired. Unfortunately the gas supply took a little longer and cooking had to be carried out as best as possible on the open coal fire.'

Norman Cohen, who now lives in Jerusalem, recalls the destruction of their family shop at No. 13 Bishop Street:

The Cathedral still smoking. Glass can still be seen in the nave window. This was claimed recently to have not been removed. But three men stated many years ago that they removed all the nave glass in 1940. If this is not the original glass, destroyed, it is likely to be 'Cathedral glass' a cheap form of glass placed in many churches during the war. This would make sense as it would not be good to board over all the nave window spaces as the vicar particularly needed light in this area.

After reporting back to my parents that their life's work was in the process of burning to a cinder (it was four days before the fire was extinguished due to the oil in the many hundreds of rolls of linoleum that were in the shop), my services were no longer needed so I decided to return some books that I had borrowed to a friend, Francis Wright, who lived round the corner in Dalton Road. I arrived there to find that the house had received a direct hit, my friend was dead and his mother was standing bewildered amongst the ruins! She had survived in the safest place the small cupboard under the stairs, but my friend, unable to sleep, had run upstairs to his bedroom to find a book at the exact moment that the bomb fell and ended his life. As I departed, Mrs Wright, who was amazingly composed, threw her arms around me and implored me to 'stay safe'.

The dead lay buried everywhere, and body parts littered the streets; the rescue services worked like Trojans digging people out of the rubble. One noted Rescue man, who was awarded the George Medal, was Albert Fearn. Albert recalled two young women dressed to the nines he found sitting dead in a shelter, one still clutched her powder compact. He said, 'I was left alone with the bodies. No marks or blemishes on their faces, just a substance coming out of their ears, which told me it was the blast that killed them. It made me feel so sad ... I am still haunted by the look on their faces, eyes wide, with shock!'

Sheila Ross, who now lives in Canada, remembered,

An uncle of mine was detailed to pick up body parts and at the end of the day he got home, outside of which were street shelters. His Mom was outside chatting to a neighbour when, to his horror, there was a head on the floor between the shelters... he placed his basket down over the top of it and chatted to them until he had a chance to put it into the basket and cover it up, but not before noticing that it was the head of a guy that he once went to school with.

I have heard a similar story to this when a fourteen-year-old boy was given a box to take to the mortuary in Hill Street and told not to look in it ... he did ... and yes

An unknown street in the city centre. Soldiers began clearing up and searching for the dead and the living as soon as the raid ended.

it was a head! Ron Shuttleworth told me in 2010 that his wife heard a rumour at this time of many lying dead, buried in a large shelter near Broadgate, this rumour linked to the Market hall and Owen's still persists to today. It appears that many believed that hundreds lay dead and the military decided to leave them where they were, a sort of conspiracy! The council denied this rumour in the press during the war. Ron recalled, 'The rumour rose because of a terrible smell of rotting flesh which occurred during the clear up. It was eventually traced to meat in a large underground cold-store.'

Ray Holl recalls,

On the night of 14 November we did not have time to go to a local shelter, so we spent the long night in the Anderson shelter. It had six inches of water in it and was very uncomfortable and cold. The noise of the bombs and anti-aircraft fire was terrifying and ear shattering throughout the long raid. In the morning we emerged to find that a number of people had died on the Smith's Stamping Works land (air raid shelter struck), only yards from us. A man was killed in a shelter on the forecourt of the Humber Offices opposite our house, and my friend's Dad was killed in the road. There were many casualties in the area from that raid. At school assembly the headmaster would announce the names of the boys who had been killed or injured the night before, rather disconcerting for a ten year old!

Martyn Hammond, whose house was destroyed in St George's Road, recalled to me some years ago memories of that morning, saying,

On that morning the question was where to go for help. Mother decided that with us six kids in tow, to make for the Council House in Earl Street. While making our way through the rubble, a building, I think it was the old church Bookshop, came crashing down just behind us! At the Council House we were told to go to St. Anne's in Acacia Avenue where they had a community centre. But when we arrived there was nothing there and we were told to make our way to St Margaret's Hall, Ball Hill. There we were accepted and given mattresses to lie on the floor, as my mother said, 'like refugees'. Later that day my mother, one brother and myself went back home to see if we could salvage any food or clothing to keep us going for a few days. There was talk about Jerry coming back that night to finish us off!

He continued,

About two days later my father got compassionate leave from the army to help us out. Meanwhile our house was being looted. Three bicycles disappeared from the garden shed and a load of coal mother had stored for winter had been pinched. We managed to save some pieces of furniture from the house and had them put

A photograph taken by the late Les Fannon of Albert and Elizabeth Asplin standing forlornly outside their destroyed home, 162 Eagle Street, on the morning of 15 November.

into storage for later... About four days after the blitz our parents managed to find temporary accommodation with one of my aunts in Middlesex, but it meant the family had to be split up for a while

The day after the 'big raid', as it came to be known, Lord Haw Haw appeared on the radio informing us once again of German superiority. Interestingly, Haw Haw (William Joyce) before the war lived above a shop in the Stoney Stanton Road, a base for Moseley's neo-Nazi Black Shirts. Leonard Bayliss recalled in 1989, 'I remember him holding a meeting in the Swanswell Park and a crowd of us chased him out along the Stoney Stanton Road.' Sometimes when meetings were held in the town they often ended with fistfights in the streets.

After the shock of the big raid some left the city on a nightly basis and slept in the surrounding countryside; men often stayed behind sending their families away; others left altogether. Jim Runnells recalls

my father, 'Big Jim', driving his M/C combination, went from Cheylesmore through streets littered with debris, fire engines and fire hoses, dodging ambulances, through Earlsdon and then Coundon, to take first my Auntie Meg and her infant son Tony (her husband Bill Probert, a survivor of Dunkirk, was serving in the Royal Warwicks) to the Toll Gate pub on Holyhead Road after which he returned to collect my mother, my Aunt, who was ten, and me from Lymsey Street, and took us to join them. We waited for hours to get on a bus to Birmingham but everyone had already filled up in Pool Meadow and we were just left standing at the side of the road. Eventually a bus returning from the Bull Ring stopped, and the kindly driver who said that he'd noticed us waiting there on previous trips told us that we should jump on whilst he returned to collect another load of refugees. Once we arrived in Birmingham we were able to take a bus to Walsall and then another which took us to our eventual destination, Norton Canes in Staffordshire, where we were welcomed by a genial old gentleman called Uncle Jack. He said 'I've been sat on the step all night watching Coventry burn and I was expecting you. Come on in and have a cup of tea. I've put hot water bottles in all of the beds.' Sometime later we returned to our battered city to be greeted by empty cobbled streets lined by a sea of broken bricks and a city centre now devoid of large buildings.

On the night of 15 November PC Lambert said,

I had to go back to the station by 5.00 p.m. as I was unable to do any more at home [his house sustained bomb damage]. When darkness fell there were at least a dozen fires still burning in the city. We had a warning again soon after dark and German bombers could be heard overhead, but no bombs were dropped. The German Air Force could have burned us to the ground that night had they dropped more incendiaries, as we had no water supply other than the Sherbourne. I remember in Broadgate on Christmas morning over six weeks later, smoke could be seen rising from the piles of bricks.

Mrs Coxwell recalled that she spent the most the night in their damp, cold cellar with her mother, father sister, brother and Gyp the dog and the canary. Gyp trembled with fear, 'but he never did bark, he was such a brave little dog', she said. By Oswald's chemist in Swanswell Street were pennies, half-crowns and shillings scattered outside the shop. She recalls, 'No one touched the money, people were like that, good honest people, Coventry people were always there to help one another in their time of need!'

The city was shattered but the spirit of the people was unbroken. One fruit shop in the city centre shattered by bomb blast had a sign hanging outside saying, 'Business as usual. Nuts to Hitler.'

On 16 November George VI came to see the results of the bombing and to raise the spirit of the people. At this point many desired to hit back at the Germans, to 'fight them with their own weapons' as one put it. 'Give Hitler hell for this,' was one

Service personnel pose on the corner of Broadgate, an instantly recognisable scene today.

The previous night's bombing ended the use of trams in Coventry as the system had been wrecked. These two stranded trams, one caught up with the other (not going around in pairs like today's buses), are on what was until a short time before the Longford Road.

cry which greeted the King when he walked the streets. The King stood in silence in the ruins of the old cathedral; the place where he actually stood was later marked by a mounted pinnacle by cathedral stone mason, Jock Forbes. During his tour of the city, the King was seen more than once to wave his car away, preferring to walk, to be closer to his people. 'I'll bet Hitler wouldn't do that,' a woman shouted as he walked the bomb shattered streets. The King then went to St George's church in Coundon, stopping on the way to see the remains of St Nicholas, Radford. At St George's he chatted to the many homeless there. Afterwards he went see the Mayor (Alderman J. A. Mosley) at his bomb damaged home in Kensington Road. When he left someone shouted, 'Are we downhearted?' To which came the reply, 'No!'

The King returned to the centre and continued his walkabout before arriving at the Council House, with its tattered Royal Standard flying from one of the shattered windows. He climbed the steps and then turned back to look at the gathered crowd. They gave him a tremendous cheer and then began to sing, 'God Save the King.' The King stood at the salute, moved beyond words. Mr Herbert Morrison, Home Secretary and Minister of Home Security, accompanied the King and said afterwards. 'His visit has been of the highest value. It is typical of his instant and spontaneous sympathy with the troubles of his people. It's something that Hitler cannot do and does not do; it is the difference between our free constitution and Nazi terrorism. I think that is a tribute to the people of Coventry and to the British monarchy.' In a quiet moment the King whispered to Morrison: 'I am glad that things have gone so well as they have in these dreadful circumstances.' After lunch by candlelight, as there was no electricity, the King left to continue his tour on foot. He eventually arrived in Pool Meadow and was presented to various AFS men who were using the kitchens which had been set up there. Before he left, the King chatted on the steps of the Council House and was overheard to say that he was happy that everything was being done to help the people of Coventry.

On Sunday 17 November the mayor, with his two daughters, visited a school in Leamington, where several hundred evacuees from Coventry had been temporarily housed. This was one of twenty-one such centres quickly set up outside the city after Moonlight Sonata. By 18 November electricity was available in parts of the city. Water mains were fixed and given temporary repairs with the help of the Royal Engineers, but it was pointed out that until the system was fully restored all water should continue to be boiled to avoid typhoid. Gas would take a little longer and was more dangerous, everyone was told to turn their gas taps off. It was said that during that weekend the majority of the population were engaged in repairing damage. There were 'marvels of adaptation in wood, cardboard and roof felting combined to make premises wind and weather proof'. At this point in the city there were twelve relief stations for clothing and feeding the homeless set up in the city. Also seventeen centres for food only, army field kitchens and seventeen mobile canteens. Food was salvaged from the ruins and sold in the streets off tables, cafes

The King standing in the ruins of the cathedral talking to Provost Howard about the cathedral's destruction.

opened as unofficial soup kitchens and residents with homes opened their doors to the destitute.

The people of Coventry continued to live with the shock of the events; meanwhile the national press were making noises about reprisals. The BBC suggested that the people of Coventry would be 'gratified' to hear of the raid on Hamburg. The Bishop of Coventry, however, said this assumption 'caused widespread and deep offence'. On 22 November it was written in the MDT that,

> One of our leading morning newspapers seems gravely concerned as to the attitude of Coventry's heavily 'blitzed' population towards the question of reprisals. We are not quite sure that it is the business of a London newspaper to interpret Coventry's approach to this subject... We are even less certain that we are in a position to analyse the subject ourselves. If the outside world is really concerned as to what Coventry is thinking in general, as opposed to reprisals in particular – it is possible for us to set down certain facts that will not bear dispute.

People checking the casualty lists which were continually updated on the side of the Council House in St Mary's Street.

The first of these is that Coventry is rather too busily engaged at the moment in the sheer task of living to worry very much about reprisals. If Coventry is demanding anything at all of our beleaguered forces, its thoughts are directed towards the Fighter Command. If Coventry has any complaint at all, it is that the city was left, 'to take it.' Coventry had waited in vain for the cheering sound of droves of night fighters. We know, and we have explained all the answers to this complaint: the simple truth is Coventry does not accept them. Coventry refuses to believe that night fighters are helpless on a bright moonlit night, and will refuse to believe it until someone decides the time is ripe for a demonstration.

Coventry is not bewailing its lot; it bewails only that part of it which it supposes to have been capable of prevention. The outside world may also accept our fullest assurance that Coventry's morale is very high. There has never been the slightest suggestion of panic or disorder. Today there is not even a sign of nervousness... Coventry feels that Hitler has done his worst, and Coventry knows now that it can 'take it.'

This is interesting, for the night fighter, during its short development, had been hailed as a saviour; people believed this even on 14 November, no doubt due to propaganda. The night fighter, however, in this period, despite this propaganda, was still practically useless, except for morale! On that night there were 121 night fighters in the sky; eleven sightings were made and one report of damage! Bill Gunston in his book, *Nightfighters: A Development in Combat & History*, says,

Riding their fine Beaufighters, the handful of RAF night fighter crews who had been converted to the type watched the burning cities, and helplessly they chased one 'contact' after another (they all seemed to disappear). Even if they had known that the waves of bombers were following invisible lines in the sky ... they could not have accomplished the vital final step of drawing in close enough behind, to see the enemy, identify it and shoot it down.

Then on 19 November one crew actually did it; a plane from 604 Squadron shot down a Junkers 88 during a night raid on Birmingham, part of the same sequence of raids Coventry was in. One of 604 wrote, 'The news was electrifying. For me it meant that the bombers we were sent to chase were really there!' The difference was that the planes' practically useless radar was linked to new ground radar, and it was said with luck and a good crew, maybe you could get a hit. According to R. Brown in his book *Boffin: A Personal Story of the Early Days of Radar*, from 7 September 1939 to 13 November 1940, out of 12,000 sorties sent out by the Germans, our night fighters had only managed to account for eight bombers shot down, and that was more about luck. Four more than barrage balloons. Soon, however, with improved systems and ground radar linked into them and more squadrons, the

From Coventry's excellent Police Museum, an incendiary which fell on Coventry on 14 November 1940 and never exploded. A rare survivor! Also two pieces of anti-aircraft shrapnel that were fired over Coventry; everything that went up came down!

night fighter came into its own and really could make a difference, albeit still fairly limited!

Another story of the time concerned the supposed lack of fire from the air defences. Ron Shuttleworth said,

> There is another rumour that the noticeable slackening of anti-aircraft fire during the latter part of the attack was due to some perverse order from London. Shortly after the event my father-in-law gave a lift to one of the gunners, who said that they were unable to keep going because they were so exhausted after several hours of continuous firing ... that they no longer had the strength to push the shells up into the breeches of their guns.

This lull must have got through to London, as I was told a number of years ago by the daughter of the man in charge of air defence in the city that Churchill was shouting down the phone at her father, telling him to get more shells into the air. On that night in Coventry 6,700 shells were fired at the bombers, and not a single plane hit. One plane was brought down by ack-ack over Burton on the Wold. Another rumour that they ran out of ammo, is just that; another rumour!

Because of the sheer devastation in the city the Government decided to suspend the ration; most of the shops had gone, as had the ration books. This helped the situation greatly, but as usual others tried to exploit the situation. On 4 December a revealing article appeared in the press. It was reported that: Councillor V. Wyles referred to the 'dastardly conduct' of the people from the neighbouring towns and villages who took advantage of the temporary suspension of rationing at Coventry to replenish their stocks of food at the expense of the stricken citizens. He also deplored the extensive amount of looting that had been going on.

> One incident of looting seemed to make the press a lot; an engineer from Loughborough was sentenced to three months hard labour for looting from the ruins of the cathedral. He actually picked up among the rubble a register for 1760 and took it as a souvenir; him and a few others no doubt! Other cases were more serious, a man from Sunderland was imprisoned for a year for looting out of a bombed jeweller, Edwards & Co. in Bond Street, watches, rings and jewellery worth over £50. A group of juveniles were flogged for stealing from electric coin meters in bombed out houses.

On 19 November, a short raid of HEs and incendiaries occurred over Earlsdon and Cheylesmore. Then on Wednesday 20 November the first mass burial took place on the victims of the bombing. The press reported,

> ... 172 of the bodies were buried. They shared a common grave at the highest point in the new portion of the cemetery, where it is proposed later to erect a suitable memorial. There were no crowd scenes, but about 1,000 family mourners, most of whom carried wreaths, formed in two long lines on either side of the entrance gates, through which they filed silently to the graveside, passing other graves which had been disturbed by bomb craters in the same air raid. Among those at the graveside were the Earl Dudley, the Mayor of Coventry (Alderman J. A. Moseley), and others. The Bishop of Coventry (Dr Mervyn Haigh) in his address said it was impossible to voice the sorrow which all felt as they stood at the side of that grave. The eyes of millions of people were upon them. 'This awful air raid,' the Bishop continued 'has brought us together in a common bond of suffering and sympathy in this city. We are better friends and neighbours than we have ever been before.' He urged them 'to go on to live in harmony with one another for the good of our city and our country.'

During the services a bomber was heard, and gunfire, followed separately by a Spitfire flying past. This may be connected to the event witnessed by Peter Cox, who said,

Probably a unique photograph of a yard in Holbrooks where coffins were being constructed for the mass burial.

The mass burial in London Road Cemetery. It's said at the time that guns were let loose as a lone raider passed over.

I had just closed the door (No. 9 Scots Lane) when a lone German fighter bomber flew low with guns blazing into the road I had just left. As it soared into the sky it seemed as though everyone came into the street ... you can imagine the cheer that went up when a Spitfire began to attack him. We watched the dogfight, fascinated as the two planes swirled and swooped in great loops above us and we cheered when the German plane burst into flames and dropped out of the sky.

Although I cannot find any written record of this event, Don Palmer of Alcester also recalled it. He said,

On this particular day we were on top of one of the 'Dumps' [World War One storage dumps by Burnaby Road] when we saw a German plane approaching, fairly low, but with a Spitfire chasing it with guns firing. They were gone in seconds, it seemed but not long afterwards the Spitfire came back and did a Victory Roll. We assumed that the German had gone down, but in those days it was hard to find out for certain.

As for the mass burials more were to come! On the 23 November a second burial took place when 250 were interred.

People continued to leave the city at night and in late November Mr E. H. Carter of Fillongley wrote to the *Times* saying,

It might be useful to record just now the impressions on living in a village near enough to Coventry to have its own casualties. We here are awed, humbled, exalted by our city's fortitude, are but one of the hosts for its indomitable people. At once our village organizations, long expectant, sprang to action; and those historic centres of free citizenship – church, chapel, and school rapidly improvised accommodation and communal meals. It has, indeed, been an unforgettable experience to receive our new guests; carrying their all, babes and pets; asking twixt smiles and tears for a barn or a loft or something useful from the lumber room; expressing gratitude that was ours, not theirs, to give. Some of us had worried about evacuees (miserable term!), and yet when they came we could have embraced them for coming. In spite of sorrow heaped upon sorrow, missing sons, homes gone – not one complaint did I hear from these families?

'He's not going to get us down!'– pointing to the continent of the air as the sirens wailed again. (But they will never forgive their Cathedral's destruction – nor forget their King s immediate visit.) Above all it is impossible to exaggerate the women's courage. Their men folk indeed, coming for a nights rest, off again to the factories before it was light, wore grimmer countenances, only to be thawed by the insistent cheerfulness of mothers and children... The children of all ages seem to have stood the ordeal almost unscathed... The *blitzkrieg*, in spite of (or because of its) barbarities is indeed welding our people together...

Despite death being all around, for the survivors, life continued; houses needed to be patched and furniture saved from wrecked houses as seen here, possibly in Radford.

By 22 November some areas had their electricity and water supplies restored; many more would have to wait much longer. Some had gas seven days later and they could once again use their cookers instead of their coal fires for cooking. Water was still being boiled to avoid an outbreak of typhoid. Evacuation was suddenly deemed more necessary as 2,000 children left the city. It was said at the time there was plenty of frozen meat available for those who have the means of cooking it, and also plenty of cold meat (Bully Beef) for those who didn't. Fresh meat was due within the week.

It was reported on 26 November that a small group from the Cheltenham YMCA came to the city with their two canteen vans:

All the communal feeding is based on a central supply depot in one of the fire stations, which has only been partially damaged by the bombs. Here there are about fifty-three voluntary workers perpetually engaged in cutting sandwiches, and all the water is boiled here, too. The mobile canteens fill at this centre and drive to whatever part of the town may need their services. There are dozens of YMCA, Salvation Army, Church Army, and WVS tea cars working in the town. On one occasion our two cars had to feed a shelter of 500 people, and we thought that we would not have enough to go round. Our thermos urns hold a great deal, however, and we managed it. The centre of the city is of course in a shambles ... everywhere we had to make detours through the side streets. Wherever the bombs had not wrought complete devastation, life was going on. People were to be seen shopping in many places, and shopkeepers who had lost their windows were busy boarding them up in the approved manner. 'One thing in particular struck me,' said Mr Davey, 'everybody is doing something, even if it is only to scrape among the ruins of their homes.

It continues,

Coventry people are not just standing still and saying, 'What shall we do?' They are getting on with the job. They have orders to bury all refuse, but the way they are dealing with the innumerable problems which have arisen, I don't think there is much danger of epidemics. The homeless spend the nights in the larger public shelters, having for the most part refused evacuation. We spent one night in a shelter, too. There was nothing abnormal, only the atmosphere of a large number of people sharing a long wait. Two girls fainted, but that was that. With dawn we ran out during a lull in the firing from the barrage, which had been continuous, and got our car, and were able to supply hot tea and food to the others. Only once during my whole stay did I see a real case of nerves, and that was with a small obviously under-nourished child in a very poor quarter.

Women selling bread and cakes in a Coventry street, not an uncommon sight with so many shops destroyed.

The main streets were now clear but work continued. In the background can be seen Holy Trinity Church, saved on the night by the Revd Clitheroe, his son and helpers. His message, 'It all depends on me and I depend on God', hung on the front of the church throughout the war.

'I think the whole story of Coventry,' Mr Davey concluded, 'is summed up in a Wayside Pulpit poster which I saw on the wall of a small chapel in a side street. "It is not what happens, but how we bear up that matters."' Mr Davey added a tribute to the ladies who shared the work with Mr A. E. Naylor and him, 'It was really wonderful,' he said, 'how they managed to keep so fresh all the time. When relief came midday on Tuesday we had only slept on one night since Sunday, and both Mr. Naylor and myself were dog-tired. On several occasions they took the cars out by themselves, and their cheerfulness was amazing.'

A correspondent from the *Yorkshire Post* visited, staying in what was left of the Queen's Hotel in Hertford Street. He left us an insightful report about another aspect of the city, its brave girls and the need for tea, saying,

People are apt to think of the Godiva story simply as the sensational part of a pageant, overlooking the central act that she was a brave and noble lady. But there is no such confusion in Coventry, where her tradition of courage is being carried on by a company of women and girls who have already earned a place in the heroic history of this war. They belong to the WVS and have done so many amazing things that film units have been up to put them on record. I heard about it from their chief, Councillor Mrs Hyde, who did not at all look like a woman who had not been home for twelve days. She just snatches sleep when she can on a camp-bed drawn up alongside her desk and its telephones. 'Looks more like

Despite everything everyone was going through it was often said people still smiled, as this AFS man from the London Laundry site on the Stoney Stanton Road proves. He had something to smile about; he, unlike some of his squad, was still alive!

Jumble sale than an office, doesn't it?' she said. Warm clothes made by their army of a thousand knitters were stacked in one corner, boots and shirts from America in another, tin hats and gasmasks in another. 'We all work here day and night,' she said, 'whatever they ask us to do; we do it, cutting all bunkum and red tape. For instance we run a railway canteen for the troops, we've served about 30,000 cups of tea there, with cigarettes and biscuits and it's all free.'

'Then we have a mobile canteen which we take to places where bombs have fallen, and serve tea to the rescue squads and firemen and the folk who have been bombed out. My girls are amazing. They take the cups of tea around even when the bombs are falling ... the other night we had an urgent call from the AFS Station. The men were taking a short spell and they wanted some tea badly. So we made it and took it across diving through the bombs.' All the time we were talking the staff kept coming in for instructions; a car driver to take some bombed out people to their billets, a shelter marshal to report, a typist for copy... The girls mostly in their teens, all pretty, the kind who in peace-time would be going to dances ... breaking young masculine hearts. 'Yes,' said Mrs Hyde, 'my staff are noted for their beauty.' Film producers come here, watch the girls at work and say: 'What profile! What grace!' It's all bunkum that if a girl's pretty she's no good. The better-looking a girl is the braver, I've found.

It continues,

For these girls of nineteen to twenty-five have gone where Hitler's bombs fall in working-class streets, they have looked stern tragedy in the face and have not flinched. Mrs Hyde went on telling the endless list of their duties. One day a group of them delighted the town by turning out with handcarts, shovels and brooms to help sweep up broken glass and debris from the pavements. Within two days they collected and supplied all the blankets and clothes needed by the women and children evacuated from the town. They supply clothes to all who need them. 'Our marshals were going round shelters one night,' said Mrs Hyde, 'when they found a new-born baby wrapped up in all the old things the mother could grab. Some girls darted across to headquarters – there was a raid on – and soon fitted that child out in new baby-clothes, every piece of which came from America.' Some Coventry people go to the shelters as dusk falls, but not nearly as many as I have seen in other towns...

It concludes,

The Chief Constable, as head of local ARP is one of the most respected and admired of men. I heard him spoken about with real affection. And the ARP men are 'doing a tremendous job.' There is, amongst, 'the real local folk, a fine spirit

Pearl Hyde, later Lord Mayor of Coventry, talking to the King and Queen.

of unity in action – and, again those modern descendants of Lady Godiva set the pace. Mrs Hyde is a Labour councillor; one of her best supervisors the wife of prominent Conservative. The Home Guard is active too. I spoke with two them – young businessmen by day – and they told me how the 'Jim Crow' system works in the suburbs. At the alert, one the family goes on guard at the front door while the others stay in bed. At the approach of danger, the 'Jim Crow' rings the door bell and the family adjourns the shelter. From my hotel window I looked out over typical bomb damage. The rear bar of the hotel has gone, and across the road the bombers have damaged a lovely, half-timbered almshouse. Here Hitler killed some old ladies. You may imagine what that did to the local spirit. The hotel receptionist comes from Leeds and was eager for news of Briggate, 'Leave Coventry?' she said. 'No it's such a homely, friendly place.' That's what I thought.

Generally, bombs had stopped dropping on the city and from 1–7 January 1941 there were twelve actual siren alerts but no bombs. Then on Tuesday 8 November after two o'clock in the afternoon the sirens sounded and a bomber flew in. The German News Agency released this the following day,

> A German bomber carried out a bold and determined dive attack on an important motor factory outside Coventry yesterday afternoon. The factory was defended by a balloon barrage and strong AA guns, but the German plane flew through the barrage and attacked from a very low altitude, dropping several bombs on the factory. A factory building received two direct hits and was considerably damaged. All the available AA guns and machine guns went into action. One member of the bomber crew was wounded. The plane was damaged in several places, but returned to its home base.

This propaganda was, of course, meant to show the bravery of German aircrews, in this case Lt Hoeflinger and Sgt Major Vogelhuber and their crew who dodged the barrage and flew in at 300 feet. Brave indeed, but no mention was made that during the attack they had also machine gunned woman and children in the street! Their target, Coventry Gauge & Tool on Fletchamstead Highway, received severe damage to the roofs of the Plating, Hardening shops and the recreation club and electrical stores. Other damage was done to the carpenter's shop, the main machine shop and plating plant. This had a negligible effect on the factory's production!

The April Raids

Since the daylight attack on Gauge and Tool the city had fifty-four actual siren alerts but no major raids, mainly small attacks and machine gunning. You would probably be right to assume that people began to think the worse of the bombing was over, but that wasn't the case. The Easter or Holy Week raids were to come!

On Saturday 12 April the press reported,

> For bomb-battered Coventry it was a bad Good Friday. On Thursday night it suffered the full fury of a big scale attack by the Luftwaffe. Coventry, from experience, knows what this entails, but this city of wreckage and wanton destruction epitomises one thing – a spirit that cannot be broken. It was for the second time this week when dawn broke yesterday that the citizens of Britain's most ravaged provincial town looked out on blackened buildings and new piles of rubbled masonry – a repetition of the scene that confronted them on Wednesday morning. More were homeless. More were bomb-injured, but Coventry last night was carrying-on much damage, and again casualties may prove to be heavy.

On Tuesday 8 April the sirens sounded after nine, signalling the start of a raid which would last for six hours and fifty minutes, leaving 281 dead. Amongst them were two doctors and seven nurses and twenty-one patients killed in the Coventry and Warwickshire Hospital, which many felt was being deliberately targeted on that night. The *Aberdeen Journal* stated,

> When a hospital was battered by both high explosives and firebombs during Tuesday night's savage double attack on Coventry. Though the Nazi raiders left in their wake a tragic trail of devastated homes and other 'military objectives,' including a school in addition to the hospital, the town showed yesterday how

well it had profited by its previous experience of 14 November. Met by a flaming barrage from the ground batteries, the Nazi bombers scattered incendiaries and HEs at random, causing destruction and casualties which it is feared will prove to be heavy.

It continued,

Following a lull between the two phases of the raid, terrific explosions shook the hospital, and it was then the majority of casualties occurred. Patients were killed before they could be evacuated. Nurses on duty were injured, but the matron said that within a few minutes the girls were talking calmly together and carrying out their duties just as though nothing had happened. 'The spirit of an English nurse is something to be proud of,' she said. A number of regular and special policemen were injured in a police station which was damaged by HEs and fire. The fire services worked heroically throughout the night and by noon yesterday the major fires had been extinguished.

The Police Station in St Mary's Street was hit near the main entrance by an HE blowing a hole in the building. A. F. Matts, Cdr of the Special Constabulary, and Special Constable Frank Kimberley were killed in the explosion (fifteen other policemen were killed during the various raids). Also damaged was St Mary's Hall; several incendiaries had fallen on the lead roof, setting the upper timbers alight. Fire crews brought the fire under control saving most of the magnificent inner carved roof. This was restored in 1952–3; most of the carvings survived, but the roof itself had death watch beetle and was removed and replaced. Stains from the soot blackened water can still be seen today. Also, an incendiary fell into the Old Mayoress's Parlour (now called the Draper's Room) down the ventilation shaft and came out upon a desk and burst in flames. Henry VIII School was also badly damaged on this night as was the railway station. The Daimler, Armstong Siddeley and Courtaulds factories were the only ones hit.

On Thursday 10 April the city was still recovering when a siren alert came again at 9.40 p.m. but it seemed that the raiders were concentrating on Birmingham; then after midnight they switched to Coventry. Then, for nearly three hours, the city was attacked with an intensity that many still recall. On this night Christchurch was hit by fire bombs burning out all except the tower and spire, which was left standing alone for the second time in its history. Holy Trinity had an HE drop at the foot of its east boundary wall, the wall absorbed most of the blast but the east window was shattered and the altar damaged. Another large bomb fell by the side of the church demolishing part of the Library. Part of the Post Office building in Hertford Street was gutted, losing its top floor. The market set up in Barrack Square was partially destroyed. A cluster of HEs fell around the Hippodrome, fortunately missing it; several fell in Lady Herbert's garden,

Coventry and Warwickshire Hospital felt like it had been targeted on this night. Some of the holes actually look more like cannon shell from fighter bombers, not normal shrapnel holes!

The Grapes hotel in Hertford Street was destroyed and the son of the landlady killed. Also Christchurch was burned out, back left.

blowing a large hole in the City Wall. One bomb hit the Hippodrome but plunged through the building without exploding! A public shelter in Warwick Row took a direct hit killing twenty-eight people; one woman was pulled out alive two days later. Another bomb of the same string smashed the Crimean cannon, which had since 1858 stood pride of place on Greyfriar's Green. Radford School was completely burned out and a number of factories hit, notably the GEC in Stoke.

Philip Deeming recalled,

During the Second heavy blitz at Easter 1941 the GEC factory was badly hit with incendiary bombs. I climbed the factory gate complete with my very good First Aid Kit to see if I could be of any help. The AFS were helpless as the water supply had been destroyed and could only watch it burn. The fire was confined mainly to the factory running along Telephone Road and suddenly the whole factory wall started to sway and buckle and collapse. Fortunately it fell into the fire and as the road was not very wide, I shudder to think what would have happened to us if it had fallen the other way.

Len Tasker recalled,

We were at the Lyric Cinema in Holbrooks when a notice flashed on the screen that enemy aircraft were approaching, however, the film would continue for those

The Council House photographed on the morning of Good Friday after taking another pasting from the Luftwaffe.

who wished to stay. My friend and I decided to stay; emerging from the cinema at the end of the film we saw searchlights piercing the sky with small aircraft dropping bombs and incendiaries. One aircraft had somehow dodged the barrage balloons and I could even see the helmeted head of the pilot in the moonlight and searchlights. I yelled to my friend to take cover and we both dropped against a brick wall for shelter. I learned later that a bomb had dropped on a shelter nearby killing the family. I also learned that an enemy aircraft had been shot down in the countryside.

Len continues, 'I was going along Foleshill Road, being near a police station I asked if I could shelter there but they directed me to the nearest public shelter. Entering the shelter I heard people singing, 'We'll hang out the washing on the Siegfried Line,' with the Air Raid Wardens conducting the singing. The defiant spirit demonstrated Winston Churchill's rallying call to fight the enemy on the beaches and in the streets.'

Harry James recalls,

During the raid someone was carried into Spon Street air-raid shelter, it was a lady and she was crying in pain. Us young children were gathered at the far end, but we could still hear the lady, it frightened some of us. As she began to scream some of the air raid wardens formed a curtain opening their coats to shield what was happening. Suddenly we all heard a baby crying it seemed a bit strange to us! But I am now aware that someone was born in that shelter at that time ... I often wonder if that baby survived.

Jim Runnals remembers the April raid as his family home in Limsey Street, Cheylesmore, was hit,

Then the first of 'our very own' stick of bombs arrived, exploding maybe twenty-five yards from the back door and severely damaged our row of houses whilst killing Ernie Colledge's dad who was an Air Raid Warden. The second bomb arrived seconds later less than ten yards from our front door and completely destroyed what was left of the roof and removed the remaining windows and doors. By all accounts there was some serious panic downstairs. Mum and Dad, covered in soot, clambered through the rubble littering the stairs seeking to rescue the bits of their tiny son and heir (me), who they found to their astonishment to be fast asleep under the stairs and unscathed. The occupants of 91 Ulverscroft Road weren't so lucky; they copped the third bomb and their house was demolished. Nos 89, 93 and 95 also suffered severe damage making my mate Roger Baker a homeless five years old refugee for the third time in twelve months. Once more we were evacuated to Uncle Jack's in Norton Canes to wait for the rebuilding of No. 4 to be completed.

UXB men investigate an unexploded bomb in Friars Road, next to the remains of someone's obliterated home. Hopefully they were in the nearby shelter (see sign). A second bomb hole is being looked into in the road itself.

Ray Holl recalled, 'I remember climbing up the railway embankment over Folly Lane tunnels when the raid had finished, to see a sea of fire, a huge orange glow, a pretty awesome sight never to be repeated.' One reporter said the following day, 'In one damaged house I saw a portrait of the Saviour and a crucifix, undamaged, hanging on one of the walls. As men passed on Good Friday, many raised their hats in reverence when they saw the picture.' This particular raid was short, lasting only two hours and fifty-seven minutes, but was particularly intensive and 170 lives were lost.

Over the two nights, thirty-three factories were bombed, including Morris Motors in Courthouse Green, which received extensive damage; the Rover test house in Red Lane was put out of action; the Daimler factory in Radford suffered severe damage over the whole site, losing large sections of the factory, including the gun turret shop and the Scout light tank shop. The Alvis factory on the Holyhead Road lost its Tool Room section and SS Cars and Dunlop in Holbrooks suffered from slight to severe damage. Armstrong-Siddeley had its machine and fitting shops, test house, saw mill, rough store, technical office destroyed and its aircraft section partially destroyed. On 11 April, Good Friday, an open air service was held amongst the rubble in the ruins of the cathedral. Then on 15 April the second mass burial occurred in the city of 394 victims of the Holy Week bombings.

On 25 July RSPCA Inspector J. T. Timms reported that during the past year 107 complaints had been received ... and there had 149 requests from various persons,

The second mass burial after the April raids; some bodies were never found!

for advice as to the treatment of their animals. Nine horses, four beasts, seven sheep, three pigs, nineteen fowls, a swan, a parrot, 417 homeless and unwanted cats. 332 unwanted and injured dogs were mercifully destroyed '... In many cases First Aid has been rendered to injured animals...'

On Friday 26 September Churchill visited with his wife Clemmie. He waved to the cheering crowds and gave the famous V sign. The route from the station to Broadgate was lined by the Home Guard and morning shoppers. Seated on top of an open car with the Mayor, Churchill smiled and waved to the crowds. He toured the bombed central area to begin with then visited the ruins of the Cathedral. Here they were each presented with a copy from the Provost's book giving an eye-witness account of the destruction of the Cathedral. They were also given small crosses made from ancient hand-forged nails salvaged from the debris of the roof timbers. The next stop was in Broadgate where 200 representatives of local civil defence units formed a hollow square, with those who had received honours forming a group in the centre. Before leaving, the Churchills visited the mass grave in London Road Cemetery. After continuing his tour on foot Churchill left, sitting atop of the car giving his V for Victory sign to cheering crowds. No one then had heard of the conspiracy nonsense!

The Prime Minister
Winston Churchill visits
the devastation.

The following day it was reported that,

> The Prime Minister and Mrs Churchill to-day sent to the Town Clerk of Coventry
> two wreaths, to be placed on the communal grave of the city's air raid dead, which
> Mr and Mrs Churchill visited during their tour of Coventry yesterday. One wreath,
> of bronze and golden chrysanthemums mingled with golden roses, carried a card
> inscribed, 'In memory of the brave and the true. Coventry. September 26, 1941.'
> This card was in the handwriting of the Prime Minister. The other wreath, made
> up of pink and dark red carnations, carried a card written and signed by Mrs
> Churchill, the wording being, 'With deepest respect to the brave men, women, and
> children of Coventry.

On the following day the Duchess of Gloucester visited the city and walked the
city streets chatting to Coventrians, and then re-visited a much battered Coventry and
Warwickshire Hospital, which she last visited when it was intact the previous November.

There were twenty-eight siren alerts on the city since the Easter raid and no
major incidents reported. Odd bombers weren't making the news; things seem to
be settling down. On Wednesday 25 February 1942 the King and Queen visited
Coventry, and saw plans for the rebuilding of the city in St Mary's Hall. The King
this time with the Queen stood in the ruins by the stone bearing the inscription:
'King George VI stood here viewing the ruins, 16 November 1940.' The Bishop of
Coventry (Dr Mervyn Haig) presented the Queen with a cross made from nails

The King and Queen chat to members of local services and hand out medals in Pool Meadow.

The King and Queen in St Mary's Hall inspecting plans for the city and its rebuilding. Note the blackened wall behind, stained with blackened water from when the fire fighter fought to save the hall's medieval roof. The man holding the paper is the city's engineer, Ernest Ford, who helped restore the hall and proposed the traffic free precinct.

taken from the old belfry. 'You have cleared up very well,' the King remarked to the Mayor (Mr Grindlay). Before they left they talked to air-raid heroes and heroines at a big ARP parade in Pool Meadow and presented some with medals. They also visited two factories and chatted to scores of the men and women workers.

Siren alerts began to die off, lasting for shorter periods every other night. Then on 30 July 1942 the city suffered its last fatalities, when three people were killed in Bulls Head Lane by what appears to be a stray bomber. These weren't, however, to be the last bombs; these fell on 31 August 1942 on the Avon Street and Alfall Road area. The bombing of Coventry was finally over; in total there were 371 siren alerts and forty-one actual raids! Many of the smaller raids were short lasting and consisted of small numbers of bombers, and generally don't appear to be recorded, making it impossible to know every raid on the city.

Although the bombing had now finished, some worried about other things. On 2 September 1943 it was reported that the Mayor of Coventry, Mrs Alice Smith, said at a conference of the Citizens Guild for Civil Defence in London that,

> As a mayor and a woman mayor ... I know that the war must be won quickly, but I do not like to see our people, so worn and pale, working in factories eleven hours and doing other work afterwards. I fear for them and I fear for consumption. We have 2,000 names on our register for houses. We are not allowed to proceed with any more housing.

She continued,

> We cannot get priority for houses for people although some are still homeless and in many cases they are living two or three families together. That, in my opinion as a woman and a mother, is altogether wrong. I think priority in providing homes for the people is as much needed as it is in providing factories for them to work in.

Alice was right, since the first bombings houses were repaired and some partially rebuilt, but few new houses were built to provide homes for those bombed out! Wartime was difficult for everyone!

I was told many years ago that for days leading up to D Day in 1944, Four Pounds Avenue was full to its whole length with tanks and military vehicles waiting to head south for the push. Winifred McCartney also recalled that Fletchamstead Highway was lined with tanks and military vehicles on the lead up to D Day.

At this time there were plenty of American troops in the city; I was told there was a small camp of black American troops in Sandpits Lane, Keresley. By all accounts they were treated better by the locals than by their own fellow Americans. George Jeary told me a number of years ago that local American troops were transported into Coventry to the Hippodrome to see private shows put on by Bing Crosby, Bob Hope and Glen Miller!

Some wartime accommodation was available in hostels; this is part of Keresley Hostel which later became part of Copthorne School in Copthorne Road, Keresley. At this time it boasted rooms, library, canteen, etc. and accommodated mainly older men and young women. The rest of the site accommodated Bevin Boys in Nissen Huts.

As all over England, American troops were stationed for a long period before leaving on D Day; many dated local girls, to whom they were all film stars! Kids at this time collected Yankee balloons they found in the streets. Harry James remembers them too;

The Yanks came to Coventry. I had never seen so many Americans, both black and white! Some came from a large camp at Stoneleigh Park and one day a large convoy of lorries arrived and they came to take us to a Thanksgiving Day party! About 300 youngsters let loose on jam doughnuts, ice cream, chocolate and chewing gum, etc. After, we were each given a bag full of goodies and huge white balloons, which only many years later I realised to be condoms! I became a regular visitor to the camp and hung around the main gates, with a 'Got any gum chum?' and 'Got a sister mister' on our lips to every Yank who came through the gates. Then one day it was deserted. We got into the camp and soon our pockets were full of souvenirs; that is until a jeep full of military police stopped us. We were taken in front of the commanding officer and threatened to be shot as looters. Then, taken to the main gate, we were warned not to trespass again ...

Two American soldiers walking down Jordan Well with the Council House in the background, probably 1944.

American troops marching through Broadgate.

then given chocolate and gum and a big wink from the last G.I. I heard the word D Day ... they never came back!

Don Palmer recalls,

We began to see a lot of American servicemen around Coventry. All the kids loved them; they were very friendly and generous with candy, chewing gum and fresh fruit – things we had not seen since the war began. Also when the Americans came we began to see a build up of military vehicles, like tanks, trucks and jeeps. They were parked on every spare piece of available ground and on the sides of the roads on the outskirts of the city. We did not know it at the time but this was the build up to D Day. Large areas were fenced off with wire fences holding rows and rows of bell tents. Not long after they left we began to hear about D Day.

One day, as Philip Deeming recalled,

I and my work colleagues became aware of a deep droning sound in the distance, which was getting louder. We all rushed to the windows to see what was causing this and saw a lot of black specs in the sky some distance away. As these specs came nearer we realised that they were aeroplanes. The noise got louder and louder and suddenly the sky was full of bomber aircraft – ours! I have never seen so many aircraft in the sky, it was black with them. We were all excited – was this the prelude to 'D' Day? The date was 6 June 1944 and our guess proved right. What a spectacle. Did they pass over Coventry on their way to Germany deliberately as some sort of gesture? Whatever, what a great moral boost it gave us. It was the start of the end ...

On D Day my Dad landed on Sword Beach with 41 Commando. A well known film of this is often seen when the landing craft approaches the beach and its scatter of houses, amid smoke and gunfire and the troops clamber off!

Soon the war ended and Coventry celebrated VE Day with street parties and dancing in the streets. George Jeary recalled to me a number of years ago,

When VE Day arrived my father, who was in business at the Brookville Stores, Holbrooks, along with my mother, was asked by Mr Stevenson, the owner of the Lyric cinema, for the biggest Union Jack that my father could get. My Dad went to Birmingham and came back with a car-load of union jacks, including one outsized one for the Lyric. The union jacks sold like hot cakes, people were queuing for them. VE Day saw me and the entire Youth Fellowship of the Lockhurst Lane Methodist Church enjoying a dance around a bonfire at the rear of the Brookville, a ruined and bombed out cinema. My mother provided

A very happy group celebrating VE Day in Benson Road, Keresley.

Celebrating VE Day outside the Wallace Pub in Keresley Road.

VE Day service in the old Cathedral.

the sandwiches. Being the owner of amplifying equipment I was in demand at several street parties. Three come to mind; Sunningdale Avenue, Freeman Street and Glover Street. There were no street lamps, no lighting; it had to be arranged, taken from the houses. Trestle tables were borrowed and with prior permission from the Police the streets were closed by them. The Sunningdale Avenue party had Christmas tree lights put in the trees. Everyone sat down to a great feed with party hats that the residents had found adorning their heads. Weeks before, the wives of the streets had stored food, made jellies, etc. The party in Sunningdale was followed, when dusk, with a film show for children and a dance for the grownups. The local bobby joined in too!

Reasons

War was over in Europe and many Nazis were put on trial at Nuremberg and executed for war crimes. On Wednesday 13 March 1946 it was reported that Field-Marshal Kesselring, former Chief of the German Air General Staff and later Commander in Italy, told the Tribunal at Nuremberg yesterday that German photographs showed that the bombing of Coventry was 'perfect'. Kesselring said, 'I was happy that Coventry was selected as a target, as it was an important military objective and was not to be hit by a terror attack. I myself examined the preparations. The night was clear and flying was easy. Missing the target was practically impossible.' Kesselring may have chosen to believe this at this time, but obviously some of his crews didn't on the night of 14 November! Kesselring was found not guilty!

A couple of days later it was further reported that Goering himself said that,

Although the Fuehrer wanted London attacked, I chose Coventry as the target because information told us that in and around Coventry the main part of Britain's aircraft industry was located. Birmingham and Coventry were the most important targets, but I decided Coventry because it had the greatest number targets in the smallest area. I planned the attack myself. I decided to wait for a moonlight night for Coventry attack. The city had been hit because the dispersal of factories, and fires caused most the damage. Look at Germany today and you can see what fires can do, he said.

Goering was hanged!

Official statistics released on 11 October 1944 of air raids on Coventry between 18 August 1940 and 31 August 1942 showed that in the first concentrated attack on the night of 14–15 November 1940, the Luftwaffe, in twelve hours, dropped 1,200 high explosives, approximately 50,000 incendiaries (other sources say 30,000) and fifty parachute mines, this being the first known occasion that parachute mines

This is Goering's reason for bombing Coventry on the 14th; the city's aircraft industry. Here we see Whitley bombers being built at the Armstrong Whitworth Aircraft factory in Baginton, at the time the biggest aircraft production centre in the city. It was likely to have been Whitleys that bombed Munich. Ironically the factory never received a single hit!

were used against Britain. People known to have been killed in the raids on the city totalled 1,252, while 1,859 were injured.

Further facts released in August 1945 state that,

> During 43 air raids practically a square mile of the city centre was destroyed, including the Cathedral, many churches and historic and public buildings. 54,373 dwelling houses were severely damaged (3,882 beyond repair), together with over 2,000 shops, seven large central restaurants, ten schools, twenty-seven licensed houses, including the two main hotels, destroyed. The Government spent £130,000 in clearing up the debris, but so far nothing has been done towards rebuilding the shopping centre on a permanent basis. The only re-building has been the erection of temporary wooden structures, with corrugated iron roofs, on sites of former shops where possible, and also along a new thoroughfare, Corporation Street, most of which had not been developed up to 1939.

It continues,

> As regards dwelling-houses, just over 100, which were partly erected when war stopped building, have been finished, and bungalows, in which no woodwork was used, have been put up. Of the first allocation of prefabricated dwellings only a few have yet been erected. Meanwhile the Corporation have nearly 10,000 people on the waiting list for Council houses. As a means of affording some relief one

One of the temporary shops in Corporation Street; Jones moved here after being bombed out.

of the largest of thirteen National Service hostels is being taken over and will be converted into flats. This hostel has accommodation for 1,000 munition workers and forms a self contained community centre, complete with dining hall, retail shops, reading and writing rooms, and a concert or dance hall. The Mayor (Ald. G. E. Hodgkinson) referred to the Corporation's housing plan in an interview, and said facts before the Housing Committee showed that, in addition to the houses destroyed, provision would be made for further street clearance and the demolition of other houses to make way for the reconstruction of the city centre. The five-year housing plan submitted to the City Council is by the Mayor estimated, including cost of land and services, at £24,651,000.

Hodgkinson, a conscientious objector in the First World War and a staunch unionist was one of the major figures in the rebuilding push which ignored ancient buildings; they were destroyed en masse in the name of progress!

The war was over and Coventry was looking to the future, then on Friday 16 May 1946 a 500 lb bomb, dropped in the 1940–41 raids, began ticking as it was rushed through the streets of Coventry by a demolition squad and detonated on the outskirts. The bomb had just been lifted from its 23-foot shaft when it came to life. This wasn't the last one; war may have ended but not for Coventry's UXB men!